Itchy, Brown Girl
Seeks Employment

Itchy, Brown Girl
Seeks Employment

Ella deCastro Baron

SD
CWP

SAN DIEGO
CITY WORKS
PRESS

ISBN 978-0-9816020-5-9
Library of Congress Control Number: 2009900740

San Diego City Works Press is a non-profit press, funded by local writers and friends of the arts, committed to the publication of fiction, poetry, creative nonfiction, and art by members of the San Diego City College community and the community at large. For more about San Diego City Works Press please visit our website at www.cityworkspress.org.

San Diego City Works Press is extremely indebted to the American Federation of Teachers, Local 1931, without whose generous contribution and commitment to the arts this book would not be possible.

Cover Design: Chris Ferreria
Production Editor: Will Dalrymple

Published in the United States by San Diego City Works Press, California
Printed in the United States of America

For Chris, Asa, and Samaria

Contents

PROFESSIONAL EXPERIENCE

FIELDWORK

HIGH ACHIEVEMENTS AND HONORS

Acknowledgments

This book took over five years to compile while in grad school and beyond, so it would follow there are many to thank who have been indispensable in encouraging me to finish this project (imagine how many more years it might have taken if I tried to do any of this alone—*shudder*). Before I got to this point, I had a writing coach for five years in Berkeley. Thank you, Mary Webb, for inviting me into this world. Thank you to editors Jim Miller and Kelly Mayhew and City Works Press for selecting this book to be published. Props to my writing group for generously editing the first manuscript of this book: Nancy Cary, June Cressy, Alys Masek, and Trissy McGhee. Chris Ferreria's lightning quick photographic, creative eye and deft (and yo, "def!"), discerning layout skills converged in the cover art. I love that Chris could make my itchy, brown, flat-nosed face look like art. Appreciation also to Alan Traylor for copy editing the text and teaching me, an English instructor, a thing or two about grammar! I am also grateful for Harold Jaffe and his support during the M.F.A. Creative Writing program as well as these years after. It was in Professor Jaffe's classes that my eyes became focused to appreciate "outsider art," to know that when people are sick, they can still create, and create well. Thank you, James Choung, who also provided a blurb and gave me my first "real," unbiased reader feedback. James' relational work within the Asian American community, along with his invitational writing for others to dialogue about tough questions around faith, engender the foundations a person like myself needs to start building a strong, dynamic identity.

I am grateful—and actually thriving today in San Diego—because of my family at Coast Vineyard. The leadership gave Chris and me copies of keys to an underused café more than eight years ago. While the kitchen was used to cook food for those living outside in the Mission Beach area, the storefront was trusted to a group of us to do as we had vision for. One decision we unanimously came to was to give free coffee and espresso drinks away. Why not?! Volunteers ran the café for students to study in. And some of us ran a creative arts, open mic night of music, spoken word, comedy, and whatever else people courageously shared of themselves. That season at Common Grounds Café began what our flyers called, the "free coffee revolution." Theresa Abueg, Emmet Blue, John & Michelle Hundley (and the home group) were steadfast supporters in our belief that art could change lives, and we need to create a safe space for it to grow. Since then, the open mics traveled to our church meeting site, transforming into Circle—a night of art, worship, and community. As for this book, Common Grounds was the first consistent place in San Diego to plant my feet as a writer and artist, and Circle nights affirmed that identity.

There are individuals within this local community who have also been part of completing this book. Stephanie Andrews helped tremendously by spending her hours last summer caring for our children, Asa and Samaria, in order that I might focus on the writing. Besides heaping love onto our children, she was a listening ear and encourager when I doubted the vision. Then, there is the "Hive" of strong, Deborah-like, "bee ladies"—Natalie Rodriguez, Jess Grupinski, Carolyn Wooten, Lisa Gavin, Stephanie Andrews (she moonlights) and Olivia Chin for praying me Up, babysitting, being my girlfriends when I needed breaks, and offering anything they could provide to help me meet deadlines. Hope and Chris Herrera, thank you for being there from Day One and never judging (quoting my old, cheesy lines, yes, judging, no—check out "Reprints"). The Herrera Home Group is chock full of people who continue to offer their time and hands for me to work on this. (Thank you also to the Herrera's twins, Sofia and Elias for loving Asa and Samaria whenever their mom had to work on the book.)

I couldn't have survived while sitting, typing, revising, and sipping at our local Starbucks without Gwen Jajou's text messages of encouragement. All of the Magee family—Jeff, Kristine, Joy, Anna, Rachel, and Moriah—believe in our family and always support us in prayer, with their friendship, with offers to do errands for us, and by babysitting the children to give Chris and me date nights (our marriage thanks you the most). Lauren Hasson is my mentor and beautiful, transcendent friend, and I met her while she was a member at Coast. Her group, Lifestreams, has been oxygen for me; I looked forward to the monthly Bible study and support meetings because as soon as I set foot through that door, I was submerged in a world thick with the fire of truth, the waters of healing. I always, always left those meetings a renewed, refined person. And Lauren has been a consistent current of breath directing me to soar as high as the dreams I've been trusted with.

I am thankful, just as deeply, for the family I was born into. Mama, Papa, sister Elise. My mom—Emelita deCastro Vega—for encouraging me to live with a fully-beating heart, to feel everything I am meant to feel, and to surrender to the path God has me on, trusting that His promises to bless me have always and will continue to come to pass. Her life as a survivor of brain trauma and breast cancer is a testament to that. Enrique deCastro—called Papa by his children—who shows me that it is never too late to start again. He moved back to the Philippines because all the years living with, "too many ghosts," as he once said, were no longer worth stealing his focus away anymore. Nevertheless, he still loves and calls us his dear daughters. My sister, Elise Dizon, for being an example of humility and grace—when I lived with her family in Hawai'i, they loved me as I was, and I always knew I had a home to come to after my long days of healing and trying to find my next step, or more accurately, gain my footing.

The people who have inspired most of the pieces in this book are worthy of praise. Thank you to other family members, the *tropa,* and friends who are daring enough to let me say these words (and possibly make you complicit). Thank you, Button family—Dane, Amelia, and Emily—for trusting me with part of your stories. It is my prayer that these words bring Life to those who need it. My college girlfriends and sisters, Jeannie Celestial, Maggie Flack, and Patricia Mendoza—your empathy, laughter, truth-speaking, and brave ability to take yourselves at face value inspire me to do the same when I am tempted to fake it in my writing. I am literally alive today because of Alicia Chavez and Carlos Penner. They are now married to each other, but back then, they were my enduring, forgiving roommates who did my share of chores, absorbed the stank of nas-tea, never judged my addiction to *Pinks* (Benadryl), turned me on to reality TV. They always made me keel over laughing at their slapstick when I was the sickest, most miserable I'd ever been my whole life.

Finally, I owe what can never be paid in full to my husband, Chris Baron and our children, Asa and Samaria. When Chris and I married, I knew him as a poet and philosopher. The way his brain perceives and communicates the ways of the world—from a Laundromat visit to his pilgrimage to Israel and the West Bank—turns thoughts inside out, excavating questions and muddy pearls of wisdom, finding the holy in the mundane. He is still that person, but since our children have entered our lives, other sides of his character have been catalyzed. For one, he feels everything our children feel as if they are his own emotions—wonder, surprise, want, joy. When our family sits at the table, plays in the yard, or corrals themselves in the family room to play games while I'm sitting at the computer, they are a model of profound simplicity, of living in (sometimes wearing out!) each moment. A book about parents says having a child is agreeing to let your heart go walking around outside of your body. Our children bring out more than the best in us; they bring out *everything* there is in us *at all*, and we stand close by, hoping, begging, praying it's more than enough to carry them through. This is how I am learning to write—part poetry, part philosophy, a lot of risk, and a beating, messy but straightforward heart. Chris and our children have brought this to our home; they embody what I strive to bring to my life and my writing.

It overwhelms me to look at this list and realize how seminal these individuals have been in planting, nurturing and harvesting everything to do with this book. Overall, these people have helped me develop the value that Art—whether it be writing, dancing, singing, or other ways of creating with our bodies—is actually a Call because when we create, we are reflecting how the Master Creator of the Universe designed us. When I write, I am encouraged by these honest voices to share stories, by simply being myself, so that others might find resonance and relevance. It is an exercise in love: of God, of my neighbor, of myself. *Maraming Salamat.*

Introduction

A few years ago, I was in the middle of graduate school, and it dawned on me that my financial aid check was long gone—some spent on actual school, some to live on, and some to pay for the Filipino part of my wedding (i.e. feeding and accommodating the 280 guests to my husband Chris' 20 guests—his New York Jewish side wasn't able to fly out seeing as we got married a month after 9-11). In short, I needed a *real* job. So, while taking classes, I began to apply for more tutoring and teaching positions around San Diego County. Since I moved to San Diego and didn't have personal connections or leads to get jobs, I had to update my resume and "sell myself."

In the midst of this, I got very sick. An inherited skin disease took over my body, then my mind, my spirit, my career in school, and my life. For a few years, I fell into chronic illness and the post-script demons (i.e. secondary illnesses) that possess a brain-chemically-imbalanced sicko. I became depressed, got insomnia, and then suffered panic and anxiety attacks. Being sick brought many things that were stuck inside of me out, including fundamental identity questions. Without a working body, who am I? When out of my mind tired and in pain, how do I get along and love people? Myself? What does my faith in God, after calling myself a Christian since I was in second grade, do for my situation when I'm this sick? What *can* it do?

I was walking along South Mission Beach one night, meeting a few friends for dinner, and I had a moment of total, inescapable self-pity. I just finished cursing my life, cussing out God for leaving me like this. I was annoyed at my Christian friends for redirecting me to the book of Job in the Bible, likening my sickness to Job's challenge to remain faithful to his trust in God. None of it helped in the least. I started to listen to the waves, and in a rare moment, my brain shut off. Without the howling monkeys to beat me into the ground, I genuinely heard something. Inside, I heard, "Record this. Write it down. It's how you'll find life." I began weeping. I knew I had heard truth. I walked to my friend's apartment, wiped off my eyes, hugged everyone there, and understood my life would not be the same after that night. I was given a directive, a mission.

I began to record these struggles, many with neither answer nor resolution. Just more questions. Meanwhile, I was a newlywed, I was not finished with graduate school, and I still needed a job. Although my skin disease certainly was not going to end in literal death for me, I could empathize with those around me who had to weather emotional and physical death sentences from such brokenness as divorce and cancer because I was also under threat of being killed—of health, of hope, of a future, of normalness.

I was still sick—getting sicker each day, actually—but my eyes and ears had new stimuli to heed. I had purpose: find the Me in the Mess. To complicate things, if you tie this chronic illness to the boat tugging along, freighting my disenfranchised, ethnic roots, you find even more questions of true, unified identity and where it can be found, earned, or if all else fails, surrendered to.

I am a first generation Filipino-American. This means my parents emigrated from the Philippines to the United States. The Philippines is a Third World country always endeavoring to become one full of Western, First Worlders. My sister and I were born and raised in the U.S. Like most immigrant families, we lived a very Filipino life inside our house, but outside, we strived to be as American—and therefore accepted—as possible. Unique to Filipino-Americans, however, is that some of the very "Filipino" ideas that we learned from our parents (like driving an expensive car, charging debt on credit cards, and buying everything name brand while still boasting great deals) were values brought from American colonizers and teachers to the Philippine classrooms way before my parents knew they would end up in the States.

But since this isn't a sweeping history book about where Filipinos came from, nor is it a typical immigrant-American story of assimilation, for the purpose of giving context for this book, a few characteristics of our people should be shared. With ninety million in the Southeast Asian, Philippine archipelago, six million in the United States, one million alone in California—the second highest population of Asian Americans in the country, we're definitely Here. You may not have noticed us because for one, we have been traditionally known as an "invisible" people. Here in the U.S., we'd been dutifully lumped into the whole group of "model minorities"—Asian Americans. (However, lately, especially in these last years, we've been starting to resist this mold. Instead of behind-the-scenes hospitality workers, medical professionals, accountants, and expert but humble billiard players and bowlers (!), we are now starting to show our faces, making our moves as dancers [from ballet to innovative street dancing], chefs, singers, professional athletes, and other polyphonic voices of our generation.)

For another, we've also been marked people of "bastard identity" because we're not sure from where our true ethnic roots originated. Because of our long history, we've got almost everyone's blood in our veins (Spanish, Chinese, Japanese, Malayo Polynesian, American, British, Asian Indian, Arab, European, and so on).

When Spain colonized the Philippines for three centuries (the islands are named after King Philip II of Spain), the Spaniards brought us the Christian faith, notably Catholicism. My dad practices this religion, as does most of the Philippines, but I was raised by my mom as a Seventh Day Adventist, a Protestant religion. After the Spanish-American War and our fight for independence (secured in 1898 in my proud dad's hometown of Kawit, Cavite), Spain annexed our archipelago to the United States. Soon after, the Philippine-American War began, and another chapter of our struggle to maintain our own, singular identity was started. The U.S. continued to bring Americanizers and Western ways of life to the Philippines along with, of course, very American military outposts.

Through the centuries, Filipinos have been migrating to the United States for many reasons, including working for Spain in the earliest years, farming land alongside Mexican brothers and sisters (Mexican-Americans César Chávez and Dolores Huerta, along with Filipino-Americans Philip Vera Cruz and Larry Itliong, co-founded the United Farm Workers), getting an education through scholarships, enlisting in the U.S. military in exchange for citizenship, escaping corrupt government in the Philippines, and trying to see for themselves if they can achieve the American Dream *in* America.

What adds to this struggle for Filipino-Americans to find out who we are is that the United States took quite some time to recognize the American part. We were called "aliens" first, and then promoted to "nationals" and "wards of the state." Meanwhile, we were not allowed to own land, vote, or even until the late 1960s, marry white Americans. This created in our forefathers, and in us, a love-hate relationship with our Colonizing "home," America. We are a people finding ourselves neither here nor there, not even knowing, if given the choice, if we would choose to settle Here or There.

One last thought about our heritage. While trying to live in our constant shades of grey, we're known to respond in black and white. Wherever we are trying to root ourselves, there are cultural aboriginal and superstitious ghosts swirling about us. We often fall back on doing whatever it takes to appease any angry gods and have our lives spared. So when we follow someone or something, we often become an "all or nothing" people. In the Philippines, for example, during Easter, an extraordinary spectacle unfolds. To celebrate Jesus' death on the cross, male prisoners and other Filipino men volunteer to re-enact the crucifixion for a ceremonial procession—one plays Jesus, two others are the thieves on either side who were crucified with him—and they are literally nailed through the hands and feet on crosses. In *barangays*, or villages, across the archipelago, people carry these crosses up and down streets. And as the volunteers bleed on display, they are followed by women who whip themselves with bamboo across their backs until they draw blood.

Many question this type of devotion, and of course, the motivation behind it. For Filipinos, beyond a religious homage to their faith, what if it's a glorified self-mutilation—like when a teenager hides in the bathroom and razor cuts dashes into her leg—and a truly naïve, though misguided way to push ourselves out of invisibility and into the realm of 3-D?

Philosophical theorist and writer of transgressive literature Georges Bataille believed, "Only in the extremes is there freedom." I'm neither disciplined nor hardy enough to willingly torture myself in order to see if I can be liberated. But in these pages, you'll see I don't have to pierce, cut, scratch or flagellate myself. The eczema and the accompanying turmoil carry me, nailed down, to these extremes. In a way, the skin dis-ease is also an ethnic ailment. What shade of brown will my body finally settle into? Hopefully, we'll see if what is found in those outermost, peripheral states of being, forced away from (what is supposed to be) a Centered life, is worth the abandon.

In the early 1990s, during my undergraduate college years, I took a rare elective, Filipino-American Literature, from highly acclaimed literary scholar (and Filipino), Oscar Campomanes. At the start of the semester, he told us two things. First, he told us we had to pay a lot for imported texts because most Filipino-American Literature was published in the Philippines. Save for a small number of well-known Filipino writers like Bulosan, Gonzales, Rosca and Hagedorn (all who were born in the Philippines and emigrated to or later visited and worked in the U.S.), there were hardly any books by Filipinos and/or Filipino-Americans published in the United States. And there were even less by Filipinos born and raised in the U.S. (In fact, that year, I couldn't find any in the bookstores.) Sitting in that lecture hall, I told myself, if I could ever add some thoughts to this modest shelf somewhere in a library, I would try.

The second thing that he offered as a caveat was how literary critics viewed the canon of Filipino Lit. He shared an excerpt from one

critic who bluntly complained that all Filipinos can eek out is short stories because we don't have the fortitude to write longer pieces. To that
prophet, I say *Salamat,* or "thanks!" This feeling of perpetual exile, of
being willing but unable to completely conform to the Western, novel-
writing culture has turned sincere attempts and false starts at telling a
story into avenues for me. Not knowing how I'm *supposed* to write gave
me the floor space to try walking the line of all kinds of "small-like-
me" genres, even to hopscotch around traditional ones, just as I bounce
around our many identities. Maybe these non-novel texts are a much-
too-late response to that Critic, but frankly, I have yet to forgive or forget
those words.

So how should you read this?

Read it as you would someone's Curriculum Vitae, from beginning
to end, or in whichever order you want to find out about a potential
hire. This is a collective text of prose, poetry, essays, e-mails, stories, and
other written forms in response to trying to find employment, or meaning, while being sick in my skin—**my itchy, brown skin.** The individual
pieces are written to stand on their own, and some are straightforward
narratives while others ask you to slow down a pace, see if there's room
to appreciate their meditative, abstract natures. But they all do hope to
find resonance and more profound connections to each other and to the
person behind the CV. Unlike reading a CV, indulge in many breaks to
go surfing, take a nap, hike, "munge," watch "Top Chef" or "Lost," and
hopefully, open e-mails reconnecting you to grade school friends.

It might serve you to keep in mind that it's an ironic Curriculum
Vitae; these are parts of an identity journey that no one admits to or
includes in a real CV. It's all the junk, the process, the stuff a sane person
wouldn't dare share with a potential employer. The "Background" section
introduces a person of immigrant parents and her hyphenated-American
identity. It also begins to unpack an identity infused with an imperial-
ized Christianity and Western culture centuries before reaching the Land
of Milk and Honey. The other sections also mimic those of a CV. "Education" continues to show initial exposure to some of the foundational

markers of my belief system while "Professional Experience" reviews how these beliefs were tested by taking them to the streets. In "Fieldwork," everything I thought I could count on is forced to bear witness when a friend who is dying of cancer lets me walk the journey alongside her. Finally, in "High Achievements and Honors," I highlight accomplishments that I've "earned." These include striking victories, equally impressive defeats, and the confused honor of vacillating between both limits. As the pieces within each section are thematic, they are not always chronological. Therefore, to facilitate this, I have included a brief timeline of salient moments in my "career."

In case you read this and think, "Hey—I know that person she's writing about," or even, "Hey—I think I'm that person she's writing about!" allow me to explain. By and large, this is a creative nonfiction collection. Most of the life events are true, and many of the characters are myself and people in my life. These individuals have courageously given me their permission to share whatever parts of their stories appear here. Many of the characters, on the other hand, are composites of people who have been integral in building this CV. Some of the points of view and presentations are my attempted ways of perceiving and interpreting prominent moments, seasons, and people in my life (e.g., God does not bake cookies and make them humans—or if he does I can't prove it, I'm not a doctor as it says in "Diagnoses," I didn't try to solve the Grand Unified Theory in college, and even though I, Ella, wrote the piece "Kaua'i," it is from the point of view of Chris, Ella's husband). And, I have to say, there were hundreds of points while assembling this book when I thought, *I wish I could say more about that time,* or, *I wish I could include those friends in here,* or, *I wish I could explain more about certain people's stories* (there are decades of history and context leading to my parents' dissolution, for one, that are not able to be included here). However, since this is a story about one person trying to present herself, please understand how the parts work to elucidate the whole. I have no doubt that the other stories and characters will have to be shared another time, another place, and more likely by other, more representative voices.

To be clear, I'm not proposing I have all the answers to basic questions of identity. Mainly, I'm just trying to learn how to speak above a whisper here, get my pipes going, see if there's something worthwhile in these lungs.

If what you read interests you, and there is a position in your organization that may be suitable for and will be supported by my qualifications, I would like to set up an interview to further discuss the prospect of working together.

I appreciate your time and look forward to hearing from you soon.

Sincerely,

Ella deCastro Baron
Itchy Brown Girl

Enclosures

A Brief Timeline
of Relevant Life Events

* 1971—Born in Oakland, California; moved to Vallejo shortly after

* 1989—Graduated from Vallejo Senior High school

* 1991—Parents' divorce announced as final

* 1989–1994—Attended UC Berkeley; graduated with B.A. in English Literature

* **Summer 1995**—Went on Christian missionary trip to the Philippines

* **Fall 1995**—After the trip, had Yosemite waterfall accident

* 1996–1997—Worked in San Francisco's Mission District for Americorps

* 1997—Experienced my first full-blown attack of eczema on entire body

* 1997–1998—Lived and worked in Oahu, Hawai'i while trying to heal

* **Summer 1998**—Returned to Berkeley, healed, and applied to graduate programs

* 1999—Moved to San Diego to begin M.F.A. program at San Diego State University

* 2000—Began experiencing second whole body attack of eczema

* 2001—Got married and more sick, continued to pursue Eastern and Western treatment

* **Beginning of 2002**—Quit the graduate program and part-time jobs, entered rehab facility for illness, changed diet and lifestyle drastically

* 2002–2004—Returned to graduate program, still sick from secondary illness (insomnia), began cataloguing chronic illnesses of self, friends, others

* 2004—Graduated from SDSU with M.F.A. in Creative Writing

* **2004–present**—Organized Curriculum Vitae; began looking for a job

Background

First Miracle

He pours water from a glass into a silver-plated pitcher and prays and prays, with his hands sweeping invisible cobwebs at the ceiling, trying to get a clearer channel to the heavens. Another pastor swings his arms high and low, sweet chariot, bellowing out *"thankya lawd thankya lawd in advance"* for answering our *"humble prayers."* I barely see over the wooden pew back in front of me, being only five or six years old. Occasionally my neck needs a strain-break, so I look over at my Sabbath school girlfriend, she at me. She asks me why my eyes are slanted up at the ends. I point to her ears and ask why there are toothpicks in the earring holes. We both shrug together. She pats my lace butterfly sleeve shoulder (courtesy of the Spanish fashion influence on the Philippines and hand-me-downs from immigrant cousins) and I point-touch my finger at the ends of her all-over braided hair. Some girls at the military base school have different colored beads at each braid's end, but the girls at our church always have tiny pieces of foil instead.

It should be the end of the service—every week it changes, depending on the weather outside or the way the preacher clears his throat before each sermon or maybe the groundhog finds his shadow and prophecies three more hours…he tilts the pitcher out and over, and what do you think spills out but red, red wine? The girls at my sides clap with me, and we smile big thinking, *wow*, this is how they felt when Jesus did it the first time at the wedding!

It is harder than usual to walk past the pastor at the door. I don't think I'll get to shake his big, root beer-colored, tough-skinned preacher hand this time with so many of the other brethren patting him on the back for his demonstration of faith.

It won't be until I begin middle school that I'll realize we are the only non-Black family in our church, and that it isn't really "normal" for most churches to have more than one color of brothers and sisters under one steeple.

It is quite a day for a miracle.

The Baker's Dozens

A twice-told tale about how God created Filipinos

God was baking cookies in his oversized self-cleaning oven, cutting out shapes of us humans. The first batch, Auntie assured us, he forgot to set his timer. They came out barely cooked, too pale to whet the appetite. So, we were told, while the ten-cup rice cooker *burble burble popped* behind us on the Formica counter, God said to himself, "I will sprinkle these cookies in Europe." Next batch, God lost track of time—maybe ten or twelve good minutes after the *DING*, putting the rest of the eggs into the catering fridge, caught too long admiring his stainless-steel reflection in the door. "Shoot," he said, half-distressed, "these are overcooked. They're dark, and they won't cool down chewy anymore." He swept his hand over them, and they fizzled invisible from the cookie sheets, instantaneously alighting on continents all across the equator.

There are variations on the last batch, because some tell it with one more bunch before the last. Auntie says with the next to last, God was rushing to set his timer, and this time he sat right in front of the oven door, its light on, so he could watch the "mass of yum" plump, spread, and begin to brown slightly. But, he forgot something *again*—the eyes—so he pulled the new population out before they could finish cooking, pressed his thumbnails in the eye spots, and angels piled them in wicker baskets, heading East towards Asia.

Finally, when he got to the last batch, he ordered his archangel to hold all his calls, summoning Moses and Elijah to answer any emergency questions that always came just as all seemed at ease, and he set to his finest batch. He set not two, but three alarms, calling Mary Magdalene to pop her head in from the sun deck when her watch read the same *time's up.* He pulled up his favorite antique stool, hand-carved by his one and only carpenter. Chin in his hands, face close enough to be warmed by the oven's blushing cheeks, he hummed the ancient hymn *How Great I Art.*

"Alas," he sighed, when the three alarms crowed and Mary nodded through the window from outside, "my perfect batch." He had to admit, he didn't plan to use almonds for their eyes, but he ran out of chocolate chips and raisins with the other batches. Almonds were all he had left. He smiled proud as punch, looking over his globe as he fanned the cookies cool with his robe sleeves. Nowhere inspiring spun into view, so he tapped once in between the Pacific and China Seas, and out sprouted one of his largest archipelagos, over 7,100 islands boiling out of the sea, *burble burble POP,* just like rice cooking.

"Ahhhh yes," God rubbed his hands together, inhaling the sweetness of his fresh-baked, perfectly browned, almond-eyed cookies. "These islands will be mysteriously fantastic for this batch—exotic and whatta place for drama! There, yes there I'll release this last multitude. I'll call them *Filipinos.*"

Balikbayan

"Maila, get me the other balikbayan box from the garage," Auntie was ordering her oldest daughter.

"Mom," I turned to my mom as we folded towels we picked up in bulk from Mervyn's, "what does balikbayan mean?" I sounded it out as I read to make sure I pronounced it right: "Bah-lick-bye-yawn." I pointed to the diagonally printed block letters on the sides of two boxes in the living room. On every side of each box it said in blue: "BALIKBAYAN BOX." The boxes were so big I thought they were perfect sizes for back-yard forts. Or, if we cut out one side, turned it upside down and sat inside, we could play news broadcasters on (or *in*) television.

My mom put a pastel yellow stack of towels into the bottom of one of the boxes. The towels were wrapped once-around with clear mailing tape. On the tape strip she wrote with indelible marker: Choleng Alcantara, 353 Orcullo Street, Wakas 4104, Kawit, Cavite. I remember it looked funny, the address all backwards. The zip code was too short.

"'Balik' means 'to go back,' and 'bayan' means 'country,'" she explained loudly enough for all of us first generation-born Filipino-Americans to hear. "It means 'to go back to one's country.'"

My dad said that our relatives needed good steak and chopping knives in the Philippines. It was too hard to find reasonably priced ones there so he had us stash some deep inside one of the balikbayan boxes. We had to hide them because it was illegal to send anything that may be construed as a weapon. He wrapped his Sears-bought assortment of cutlery with different soft things that went in the boxes. Hanes brand T-shirts, Sergio Valente blue jeans, even one of the stacks of towels my mom was wrapping in tape. What looked like tons of every other kind of dry goods went into the bottomless boxes: Hershey's chocolate bars and chocolate milk mix (a random bottle of Ovaltine); hand-me-down dresses from the backs of my sister and my closets; white tube socks with different-colored stripes at the top—the kind that spelled fashion tragedy if the stripes were green in P.E. class. Inside, on top of each of the hilt-filled 75-pound boxes was a bundle of letters and greeting cards filled with checks for American dollars (they might get a good exchange rage for pesos depending on when they cashed them) from anyone here on the Mainland who had family left in the Philippines.

And everyone had family left (*and* right) in the Philippines.

Trips "back home" were so economically tight that when they were planned, for some uncanny reason, Bay Area neighbors from all around made their mini-pilgrimages to the house with the balikbayan boxes poised to fly. We took each other's goods and made allowances for delivering presents from "strangers" because nobody knew when the next trip to the Philippines could carry their packaged love for free.

Auntie Aida and my mom were best friends in the *tropa* (group). Our specific tropa came together after all of our fathers retired from twenty years of service in the U.S. Navy. They had fought together on the same ship. Well, mostly they'd been cooks and bookkeepers, eventually sent to fight on the front lines in Vietnam when the chaos called. There were about ten families in our tropa, and who knows how many tropas in the naval town of Vallejo.

People in the tropa did everything together. A year before, in sixth grade, I had heard that Native American tribes such as the Iroquois lived communally, raising each other's children. In effect, each child had several mothers and fathers. To the best of my twelve years of historical knowledge and experience, our tropa was exactly like this.

I was scared of Auntie Aida. Even though each mom in our tropa acted as our mom when the need arose, there was an unspoken expectation in the mind of each kid that only birth moms administered true discipline, e.g., spanking and grounding. Since Auntie Aida was my mom's closest friend, my sister and I suspected that our mom had given her this privilege. I remember playing with Charlyn (Auntie Aida's middle daughter was my best friend by default because we were only a year apart in age) and getting spanked together religiously for our playfully constructive, eventually destructive "gallivanting" (a favorite English vocab word all the parents must've learned pre-immigration).

One time, Charlyn and I went door to door and tried to sell the shoes on our feet for pocket change so we could buy Now and Later candy at the Laundromat. The neighbors called Auntie Aida and exposed our marketing scheme.

"You GIRLS!" Auntie Aida would say as she raised her *bakya* (wooden slipper) and went WHAMM! on our thighs as Charlyn and I ran to the bedroom.

"You keep galli-BAN-ting like DIS, AY nako! You're going to gib me a heart at-TACK!"

We ran, each to her own anonymity. Like lemmings without reason, scattering aimlessly to the sea.

I remember the fear, but I also remember the respect I had for her. Just as "real" moms should, she never let me get away with my push-the-envelope pre-teenery.

Auntie Aida was the one going back to the Philippines this time. She was supposed to see family for the last time and bring back her father to be with her and his three granddaughters. She only had a few months left.

Years earlier, Auntie Aida survived breast cancer. Just recently, after going to the doctor to treat a chronic flu, she had been diagnosed with leukemia.

My mom sat my sister and me down the first time Auntie Aida had to stay for a long time in the hospital to explain what was happening to her best friend and our second mom. The best she could say without getting too complicated was that Auntie Aida's blood was sick.

She started talking perfect English, without much wavering in her voice.

"Auntie Aida's blood now has the cancer that they tried to remove from her breast. They took one of her breasts to try and stop the breast cancer from spreading, and it worked for almost five years, but they couldn't do the same for her blood."

She held her breath for a long second, like she was trying to material-ize enough strength to finish the conversation.

"Sometimes they can replace the cancerous blood with healthy blood, but we're not sure if your Auntie Aida can endure it. We are just going to wait."

As my sister and I started to cry, my mom sat in between us and put her arms over our lowered heads. We knew this meant we weren't waiting for Better; we were waiting for End.

My mom said that all of us kids in the tropa were to be extra-sensitive to her and to offer our help whenever we were with her. She also said that, since our family was the closest to her family, my sister and I had more responsibility to be the best friends we could to her three daugh-ters. Especially to the youngest one, who was barely six years old.

In school they never taught me about cancer—it was 7th grade. Although we learned about the body in 6th grade for Health Educa-tion, we only learned about how our bodies were metamorphosing into "adulthood." To me this only meant I would be getting my period soon, and maybe a boy would notice me as a woman with boobs instead of a girl with mosquito bites on her chest. I didn't know a thing about how the body's immune system gets paralyzed, and then disintegrates when its cells' DNA is attacked by cancer. I thought I was watching something that was an "adult thing," which is why I couldn't imagine handling it maturely. But it must have been much larger because it was almost too hard for my mom and her circle of indestructible friends to handle.

Whenever we had sleepovers at Auntie Aida's house, I would look at the back of Charlyn's head next to me in the sleeping bag. I couldn't sleep. I kept feeling sorry for her, Maila, and Wennie, who were *not* adults but had to deal with this. Somehow, I felt this would affect their own entrances into adulthood.

A long time before, when Auntie Aida had first gotten sick with breast cancer, I was sitting in Treasure Island's V.A. hospital waiting room with Maila, the oldest daughter. The doctor told my mom and us "older" children that now each of Auntie Aida's daughters would have a fifty percent chance of getting breast cancer. With this new cancer, I wondered what their odds were now.

When the leukemia started selfishly invading the tropa's time together, we saw less and less of Auntie Aida at the weekly blackjack and mah jong get-togethers. The chemo sucked the life out of her, virtually one breath at a time. Within a few weeks of beginning the different rounds of chemotherapy, she was only able to come to a few of our parents' weekly gambling nights. During the last season, whenever the parents fed their ravenous addiction to gambling (it was the "California Dream!" America, the "Land of Milk and Roulette!") by going on Reno escapades, we kids stayed at Auntie Aida's house.

The last time Auntie Aida disciplined me, Charlyn and I were eating watermelon outside of the house. We decided to race spitting seeds onto the side of the garage as we mercilessly devoured fist-sized gouges of watermelon. Well into our second round of machine-gunning seeds at the white stucco-looking wall to the left of the garage door, Auntie came outside, responding to her sixth sense that we were up to It again. She had a red scarf wrapped around her head, and she was holding a pair of pants she was sewing for some neighbors. She was wearing a red floral-printed duster. I saw her unpack it from the returned Balikbayan Box after her visit home. Those loose-fitting housedresses were trademarks of Filipino motherhood. That time though I wasn't reminded of my heritage. The wind blowing through her dress reminded me how Auntie Aida's body was disappearing, and how one of her breasts was already gone. When she opened her mouth to reprimand us, she didn't have her front teeth either. I don't remember much more about that day except that Charlyn and I got cramps in our knees from kneeling on the ground and collecting seeds and watermelon chunks.

And that, *that* was the last time we got her angry.

Through it all (when she wasn't scolding us) she never stopped smiling. Sometimes her smiles held up fatigued and furrowed brows, but they were still smiles. One time I walked into her bedroom to use their bathroom (Maila was in the hallway one) and discovered that it was the only real thing on her face. The wig she had started wearing was on the Styrofoam woman's head on the dresser, and her dentures were lolling in a glass of water on the bathroom sink counter.

During the last week of Auntie Aida's life, we tropa kids spent all of our free time at their house waiting. Waiting emptily in the empty living room with empty hopes in our laps. Charlyn and I did, in fact, turn one of the balikbayan boxes into a television. What had given us several weeks of ad lib weather reports and fits of pee-in-our-pants laughter now sat beside us on the couch. Empty, too. That time no news was Not Necessarily good news.

We spent a lot of time on Treasure Island, the military island in San Francisco that had a hospital advanced enough to deal with her sickness, but I never for a second thought that there was anything valuable or "treasured" on that island that would make anyone want to stay. As the other tropa parents played blackjack and mah jong down the street at another family's house, my mom was the one who stayed on Treasure Island with Uncle Wes. She would not leave Auntie Aida's side.

My mom came back after two straight days without coming home to change or take a nap. She went to the bathroom. My sister and I heard her quietly sobbing, begging God for some sanity to get through the next days.

"Oh God, please. Oh God, please. Please, God," was all I could make out.

She came out of the bathroom and called the Cacuyogs who lived in the same court as we did. She told Auntie Gina it was "Over" and asked her to call the rest of the tropa and meet at Auntie Aida's house.

"They did Everything. Everything," were the first words out of my mom's mouth.

Each set of parents sat or stood next to each other. Most all of them were holding each other. The dozen or so kids sat together on the carpet. I was picking at the green knots in the carpet, crying as noiselessly as I could.

My mom continued, "I have never seen any human beings as strong as the doctors and nurses that worked on Auntie Aida. As soon as she coded, they called everyone who could help and they worked as fast and as hard as they could all night and all morning. Nonstop."

My mom crumpled into tears, and one of the other moms stood up and put her hand on my mom's shoulders, trying to get her to sit down at the dining room table.

Sobbing, my mom ended, "I've never seen anyone work that hard to try and save a person. Never."

It especially amazed my mom because she worked at Kaiser hospital and had had to deal with the cycles of life for half of her waking hours for almost two decades.

There was a rosary at Auntie Aida's house everyday for nine days after that. My dad was the Catholic in our family and told us this was called *Pa Siam* meaning "nine." My mom raised my sister and me as Seventh-Day Adventists; as a result, we were two out of the ten Filipinos in the world who were NOT Catholic.

Each night at dinnertime we would go to Auntie Aida's house, and every family took turns bringing the *pancit* (noodles), *lumpia* (egg rolls), or *arroz caldo* (rice stew) to the house. Uncle Wes, Auntie Aida's husband, rarely spoke. I only saw him when he refilled the white platter with a mountain of freshly baked *pan de sal* (bread rolls) from paper bags kept underneath the dining room table.

When the eating was finished, everyone gathered around the family room. Auntie Emily led the rosaries; sometimes Auntie Chit helped her with the readings. Responsively, we were reading from photocopied books that I supposed someone had made for the occasion. I read quietly, participating as fully as a non-Catholic knew how to. I asked for beads to follow along with cataloging the "miracles" read. Even when my mom looked at me and gave me a disapproving Seventh-Day Advent glare, I didn't care.

"After the Lord Jesus was raised from the dead, He went and showed himself to those he loved," the priest said.

He explained that during the Pa Siam, we were praying on her soul's behalf that she be allowed into Heaven.

"And after forty days of visiting His loved ones, the Lord Jesus Christ left the earth. He told them He was going to prepare a place for them to live and that He would come back to get them—to get us so that we can live with Him in his homeland." The priest made the sign of the cross after the benediction, and everyone followed.

Following the last day of the rosary was the viewing. Before Auntie Aida died, she had told my mom she wanted her father to come back with her from the Philippines so he could take her back there to be buried. She wanted to be with her other family under the soil she grew up on. She wanted to go back home.

There were a couple hundred people there, crying, rocking back and forth in their seats, holding hands, asking God "Why?" over and over.

I sat awkward and silent in the front row with Auntie Aida's daughters. Charlyn was suffocatingly stoic as she had been during the entire two weeks. She didn't pray the rosaries; I could see her all those nights holding her green rosary beads. Holding her breath. Holding it in.

My mom nudged us from behind.

"It's time. Go up and say one last goodbye to your mom," she told Charlyn and her sisters.

I stood up with her, fell in line behind her, and we watched as Uncle Wes walked up to her casket. He stood there talking slowly to her in Tagalog, their native language. He kissed the framed picture of her on top of the casket. He bent low to her face, kissed her, and stayed there for as long as he could. I believe he was saying a last prayer, begging God to bring her back. Offering to trade places with her. To take the ride in the box so that she could be here with her daughters.

One of our uncles in the tropa had told us earlier that day that we should all give Auntie Aida a goodbye kiss. He said that, "when you touch a person who has passed away, you are no longer afraid of anything." Uncle Wes looked fearless as he walked away from the coffin. It was true.

I walked behind Charlyn, not saying anything, but offering as the biggest gesture of middle-school best-friendship my loyalty of presence. When she got up to Auntie Aida, she wouldn't look at her mom. I thought maybe it was because Auntie Aida didn't look like herself anymore. The sickness had made her skin several shades darker. Her wig looked like it didn't fit her. Her makeup wasn't on right. Her face was bloated. There was a smile forced onto her face, but it wasn't her smile. It was fake like her wig.

I didn't tell Charlyn, or anyone for that matter, that I thought this.

I whispered to Charlyn, "Kiss your mom goodbye like your dad did."

She didn't move. As we got a few inches closer to the casket, close enough so that we were both touching the carved wood with our chests, Charlyn bolted from my side and threw her arms into the casket. She started holding her mom around the shoulders, trying to pull her out. She was wailing now, and I froze next to the spot she was standing on, my eyes drowning in the deluge of tears.

"Noooooo!" She was yelling. "Mommy, Mommy, noooo!"

Uncle Wes got up from his seat and took hold of Charlyn's convulsing body, trying to anchor her. Charlyn was oblivious to everything, everyone. She just wanted her mom.

Charlyn's dad walked her to the back of the viewing room. He sat her down and kissed her on the forehead. I sat down beside her against the back wall of the mourning room as everybody else said last prayers, bidding Auntie farewell. Charlyn had her knees drawn up to her chest, her head buried in them, her wreath of arms circling her head.

I looked up at the bronze Jesus nailed to an also-bronze cross hanging over the doorway. He looked so tired and sad. It didn't look like he was too content to do what he did on that cross. I wondered why it had to happen like that. Why Jesus gave his life on the cross so that we could live. Why he rose after being buried for three days, and why he went back to heaven after telling his people that he was coming back to get them. I didn't ever really think this may or may not be true; it's just what I was raised to believe. I believed it was truth, but I didn't know how this applied to Auntie Aida because she *hadn't* lived.

In my sorrow and confusion, I was too exhausted to really think about this. I could only remember back to the long days of helpless second-guessing about how long Auntie Aida had left to live. I saw her emaciated body in the back of my mind, her weakened body trying to keep in step with her still-strong spirit, her ingenuous smile through it all.

And did this promise from Jesus apply to her?

Forty days after her death, the tropa met one more time at her house. They had one more rosary. Forty days after her death because that's how long Jesus lingered on earth before ascending to heaven. The family friend-priest from St. Vincent's Church, the one who had blessed their new house, spoke about letting her go, how she received true healing from her pain by going home to the Lord, and we should be confident in releasing her.

Except for my mom, I could still hear our monotoned moms and dads reciting the last part of the rosary that we had prayed during the Pa Siam, and now prayed for one last time. Over and over, we beckoned each of the dozens of Catholic saints.

"Saint Joseph, pray for us," we would admonish. "Saint John, pray for us."

Towards the end, we all repeated a prayer to Jesus, the Jesus who had risen from the dead.

"Oh my Jesus, forgive us our sins. And save us from the fires of hell. And lead all souls to heaven, especially Aida Encarnacion Copon's."

So he could do this, I guessed.

I closed my eyes, feeling a little dizzy at the repetition. The liturgy continued with some impromptu enlistments of the Virgin Mary. The "Mother of Mercy," the "Mother of Perpetual Hope"…

In the background of my nightened eyes, I could still see Charlyn grabbing at her mom in the casket, trying to keep her from leaving. Never mind that Auntie Aida was being escorted to heaven by God's very Son Jesus, she was still being taken to that Somewhere Not Here. Charlyn had been trying to pull her mom out. She'd wanted to pull her out of the balikbayan box.

Heads Up, Seven Up[*]

When my seven-year-old niece asks why
her church invites her to sing at the pulpit some Sundays,
but when she grows up she won't be allowed up there to teach
(like Ms. Arlene teaches her in the back classroom of the sanctuary
for Sunday School) I'll tell her it was a simple game
of "Heads Up, Seven Up" they played.
Squished in their second grade desks, all in their adult-sized
pastor robes, the HRIC (Head Robe in Charge) swished
up and down the aisles, looking under everyone's robes for skirts.
And under those skirts, slips, and just to make sure
(maybe to be fair), under those, panties.
We other Christians played, too, in our church clothes,
contorting our high knees around the same low desks.
And when our heads were down, rumor has it
Mr. HRIC was tripping over his own bulging eyes
at all the satin, animal print, french cut, blazing red,
even the gran'ma style "back of the drawer"
drawers, his saliva slinking down his chin all slow and sugary
like legs of dessert wine climbing down the glass.
He tapped their thumbs quick
(so they might not feel how stiff and loaded he was).

---

[*] Heads Up, Seven Up: A traditional elementary school game played since the 1950s.
The teacher would choose seven students to come to the front of class. These seven
were going to be the "choosers." The teacher would then say, "Heads Down, Seven
Up." The unchosen students put their heads down, closed their eyes, and stuck out one
thumb. The Choosers walked around the room and each furtively tapped one head-
down student's thumb. When all the Choosers returned to the front of class, the teacher
would say, "Heads up, Seven Up." Seven students would stand up because their thumbs
were touched and try to guess which of the Choosers tapped them. If the student guessed
correctly, s/he would replace that Chooser. If not, the Chooser remained at the front for
the next round.

No one told us the rules changed,
that this was a lowball game, so if you were "it"
you were really "out,"
(not tit for tat, but *tap* for *tits*).
And apparently we had all approved of the new rules
because when we looked up from our desks
we were all giving the thumbs up, too.

Another Grandfather Poem

In workshop, while culling and mulling peer comments,
one student offered feedback on the poem at hand.
"You talk about your grandfather's food, how he wore his clothes,
and how you visited him while you were young.
I can see that and all, but it's not unique enough because
everyone has a grandfather poem."
I didn't hear the other comments,
strangely offended by that particular remark.
I never had a grandfather to write a poem—
cliché or inventive—about.

Never really had any grandparents
on either side.

I remember being at a grandmother's funeral.
I was two years old, flying seventeen hours
to my mom's province of Pampanga.
Before that, I had no memory of her making *pancit* or rolling *lumpia*,
inviting me over for *merienda*, or giving me wise advice.
This *lola* lived with me only in nightmares
of brown and red splotchy faces melting from hot tears
all morning and night. *Até* Sharon held me up over the casket,
and I started crying, too,
       but only because I was afraid.
Lola's face—tiny and proper with her large Spanish eyes
and flat, Chinese nose—was mapped with wrinkles
that ran into her gray hair, tucked in a "grandma bun."

My other *lola* I saw only three times. When I was ten,
she laughed at me and pointed her small frame towards my first cousin Marilen,
gesturing through gummy laughter how we were exact twins,

one in the Islands, one in the States.
For two vacationing weeks, she told me stories in Tagalog about her son,
my Papa's deviant days. The second time, in college,
Mama announced she wanted a divorce,
and Papa revealed what she called "irreconcilable differences"
was really her affair with his Navy shipmate,
a man I called Uncle my whole life.
He was part of our *tropa* where everyone was Auntie and Uncle,
maybe because our parents needed the large families,
a reminder of their homeland.
I fled with Papa to his hometown in Cavite,
to see if I could leave the rage in California.
The last, during a Christian missions trip,
we braved three hours of harrowing jeepney rides
and black lungs from untempered car exhausts
to see *lola* for a "quick" lunch.
She was smaller than I'd tried to remember,
sitting on the bamboo chair underneath the porch's shade,
fanning flies away. Her ears are what I still see—
large clam shells, shiny and protruding, unwithered by age,
        exactly like mine.
Papa wrote me from his ship sometime later,
mentioning *she passed away the year before.*

I have never met my grandfathers.
My *lolo* on mom's side simply could not live long enough
to greet all of his six children's progeny.
I don't know what happened to Papa's dad,
my other *lolo.*

This comment lingers long after workshop.
I recall the poem our classmate turned in,
become desperate to run the risk of falling into routine,
to have someone accuse me of the "heard-it-before" crime
of having a "grandfather poem," too.
I suppose when Papa came with the wave of recruited Vietnam soldiers,
and they left their homes to fight and live as Americans,
they left *my lolo,* and all the poems about him,
somewhere out there under the porch's shade,
listening to *lola* chatter blithely
about Papa's gallivanting days.

Jesus Action Figure

"Knock, and the door will be opened to you."
—*Matthew 7:7*

I asked Santa for a Jesus I can see.
Christmas morning, my big sister and I ran
to the silver-foil pine tree we recycled year after year.
Mama saw me look at my unfilled stocking,
led my eyes below it onto the fireplace.
She pointed out my special present.
My Jesus Action Figure had poseable arms
and gliding action under his feet.
I wondered if, in the bubbly bathtub lake,
would he have floated across to the spout,
grabbed the hot and cold handles, one in each hand,
and raised himself up like a gold medal gymnast doing an iron cross.

My Jesus was "manufactured in China"
where they poured resin into the mold for his long,
root beer colored hair and flow-frozen robe.
They labeled him part of their *accoutrements toy division*,
packaged him against a cardboard mural of old Israel,
the nation's manmade walls still impervious,
enemies lurking on the other side.

"Lights out," undercovers, I ask Jesus for wealth.
Later, when I'm at the hospital again for more steroids
to treat my bleeding rashes, I find I want health instead.
I beg Jesus to help me seek knowledge.
When I learn bigger words from watching late night news,
I lament what I read and see.

I knock and knock,
but I can hear no answer this side of the plastic packaging.
I can see Jesus' coarse, painted-on waves of hair.
He looks past me with sleepy eyes, lips heavy at the corners,
open palms curled at me. I pick up my action figure and shake it.
If he can't hear me knock, maybe he can feel my trembling.
Mama catches me, reprimands at once. "That toy will be a collectable one day!
Don't bend it or take it out of the box! It's worth more untouched."
She picks Jesus up and puts him on top of the highest shelf in the china cabinet.
He's there, next to all of our cousins' wedding favors, my sister's spelling bee trophy,
holding fistfuls of dust, faithfully waiting.

Archipelago

"I love visiting San Diego, but I would never live there." I got this from over half of the casual conversations with people from home that had come a few times for vacation. I also got, "It's a bit claustrophobic because you only want to stay at the coast. There's really nothing inland." This from recent transplants to the San Diego area.

I made my list.

> *Compromise: It was only an hour and a half plane ride from Northern California, and I could visit my mom and friends I had made while living in Berkeley and working in San Francisco and the Bay Area anytime.

> *Pro: The ocean was definitely no further than any ten-minute drive off of any west-bound I-5 exit. I could find a place close to the arterial freeway.

> *Pro: I could work for the disenfranchised in any school part-time. In addition, if I wanted, I could go to Mexico to work and to learn the Spanish I never learned in high school and college (French sounded so pretty, useless as it is to me now since I live in the state where Spanish is the first language of about half of those living in it).

> *Compromise: The characteristic Bay Area progressiveness and the rampant in-your-face social activism of Berkeley might have to be cultivated or sought out through casual and deliberate verbal want ads, but like a match head struck on a rough surface, the mere presence of a community of people sparks the need for response to the human condition. I could align myself with the majority of people who want to evolve rather than devolve.

I went to the Torrey Pines Reserve beach before I had to drive the ten hours back to Berkeley. I remembered some advice that, when in doubt, I should get as quiet as I can and pick away all the voices in my head, all those nagging moms and paranoid friends, turn off what the writer Ann Lamott calls "radio station KFKD," and I should listen as long as it takes for the One voice that's left talking. I would know this voice by its clarity and its conviction in ending all sentences with periods.

The veil dropped. I called San Diego State's graduate program and accepted. I already had most of my post-Hawai'i things still half-packed or given away so my truck carried a Diet Life: me, a futon bed, a basket full of clothes and shoes, a box of books, among them imported Filipino-American literature from a rare class at UC Berkeley that I treasured, and recorded tapes of drive-along songs from my friends in the Bay Area.

℘

My idea of camping was driving thirty minutes to the State Park, backing the Volvo station wagon into the parking space between the two planted trees so we could sleep in our Sears bags in the back of the wagon, and eating cold Filipino food over rice under the raised back door of the Volvo while our parents played mah jong or blackjack under the stars. They packed a card table and Hoyle gambling chips and left any form of hiking boots at home.

I was raised in a naval town half an hour north of San Francisco. The population of the town appeared to be fifty percent Filipinos, forty-nine percent African Americans, and one percent Caucasians and Mexicans. My father got the ticket to America that his brothers were promised in the Philippines: fight for the USA in Vietnam, and we'll give you citizenship to our country. Waiting for a visa has taken most of our relatives up to twenty years to be approved, and he was nineteen years old and hungry. My mother got a scholarship to study medicine in Florida where she met and married my dad. By the time I was born, dad was on his way to retirement from twenty years of service to the U.S. Navy, and we were buying our first home in Vallejo, California. We moved once to a two-story house closer to the Napa side, and that's where I stayed until I was eighteen. My sister's and my upbringing could have been the fifth story in *The Joy Luck Club*; even though they were Chinese Americans, we were under the same cultural lock and key, wearing the same blinders.

My parents coveted the American Dream. The twist was my mother and father's idea—beyond raising us while providing all the opportunities to succeed that they, our parents, missed growing up in a Third World country—had little else in common. As this trenchant reality set in through the decades, the entity called "our parents" eventually began to unravel. From the outside, as our parents further disengaged, some family and friends in our tight community began harshly concluding that my mom seemed to view my dad as a stepping stone to attain the American Dream for herself. This was not unlike how the United States Navy used him as its meal ticket to cook and balance books on the ships. From where I stood amidst secretive hushed words, midnight sobs, and distant glares, I couldn't figure out what or who was to blame: the Dream or the dreamers.

When I left for Berkeley, mom left dad for another man who joined the Navy under the same promises as he, came from the same province in the Philippines as he, fought on the same ship as he. My one, older sister finished college, married her high school boyfriend, and moved to Oahu, Hawai'i.

I finally went *camping* camping with my friends in college. I was addicted. When I graduated from Cal, I had begun backpacking through unmarked territory all over California. It seemed I had finally found out how to get the ghost of my parents' archipelago, over 7,100 islands in their country—7,100 seeds they inadvertently planted inside of me—off of my conscience.

Cue Yosemite trip.

I was known as the "girl who fell down a waterfall and walked, or hopped away, to tell her story." In 1995, I got myself lost backpacking in Yosemite National Park's Tenaya Canyon. I was first aid trained, but I was a wilderness survival dolt and knew nothing more than what a Ricky Schroeder movie called "The Earthling" taught me: if you follow the water downstream, it always leads to people. I believe it was God's way of recalling my collective knowledge throughout my twenty-four years of life. He must have surveyed my pathetic acumen of latchkey kid TV trivia, precocious gambling skills, distilled university knowledge, my face-making talents to accompany the odd characteristics friends called, "uniqueness," and a dozen or so church songs from Christian Vacation Bible School, and took pause. After a quick shoulder shrug, He gave me the clue to follow the stream I was drinking from. I remember the movie *The Earthling* and how little Ricky, lost in the forest as well, found his way to civilization. However, in the version I saw, no one mentioned the stream turning into a powerful, stone-chiseling cascading waterfall so steep I couldn't see what was below me—there would be a pool of water somewhere at the bottom, but *where would I land?*

I got stuck on one side of a mounting cascade and its freefalling counterpart, a waterfall, for hours. No strength to climb back up the face of the rock that took me half a day to inch down, and just when I began to ask God what to do (out loud and in between bursts of tears and trying to sing myself calm with kindergarten Christian "God is so good" songs) I slipped and fell. And fell. I fell one hundred and fifty feet to the bottom of the waterfall.

I screamed, "GAWWWD" all the way down. I bounced on some of the cascade rocks before the freefall. While doing so, I kept anticipating the crack of my skull being the last memory of this life along with flashes of salmon colored rocks, water, and sky. I didn't see my life flash as people swear by.

When I landed in the water, I struggled to get air.

"I'M ALIVE!" I screamed. I started to swim to the side of the waterfall but noticed my right foot wasn't kicking. I lifted my leg out of the water and saw that my foot, still in the hiking boot, was ripped off to the right, attached only on one side.

I went into shock. I swam myself to shore, treated my leg as if it were someone else's, elevated it, and cried. After an hour of helplessness, I decided I would do what I had seen in movies. I would anchor my foot to my leg, get up, and walk the remaining fifteen miles to Half Dome where I knew there were people. On television, people get their arm caught in a vice, torn off, and then pick it up and continue fighting with it on to victory. Not the case in real life.

Hypothermic, my foot ripped out of the ankle, a sketchy tourniquet that I made with my Swiss Army knife and a shoelace from my hiking boot, bloody and bruised on more and more of my body each time I had any courage to check myself, I almost missed the rescue helicopter, the great red and white bird of salvation because by the time it came at dusk, I had already thought I heard six or seven *other* rescue planes and helicopters in my starved and weakening hallucinatory state. I had given up and huddled under a leaning rock, closed my eyes, and asked that if I fell asleep, I wouldn't wake up.

After spending the night with two paramedic rescue heroes and getting shots of morphine into my air-splinted leg, I was strapped into a litter single-strung to the helicopter, a hundred feet from its base, right as dawn came. Granted, I got an unobstructed view of Yosemite's famed Half Dome that no one else will see, but for this peek I had two helicopter rides, three surgeries, a hospital bill of over $150,000 to my insurance, and several months of severe Post Traumatic Stress Disorder. I thought it was tough trying to survive while I waited to die out there, but the worst part was the year and a half afterward. A bumper sticker says, "If you're not busy living, you're busy dying." I was certainly *not* busy living for all those months.

I tell this to people now, my chin pressed into my chest and my voice hanging on that precipice of the all-ridiculous nostalgic, "I've had it tougher than anyone, walking four miles uphill—both ways—to school in blizzard AND desert weather…" tone. All drama aside, I have found that there is no way I can dilute this experience that has marked me.

Literally, I have these marks to keep me humble. I have metal throughout my ankle because of the compound fractures in so many bones that had to be more than band-aided back together. Where my foot tore itself out of my ankle, I have a sideways "Y"-shaped scar.

I call it my Why? Scar.

My psychologist at the time told me that any kind of trauma to our bodies, physical or otherwise, sometimes bubbles things to the surface.

So there. After five years, I finally had to deal with my mom's infidelity after being a leader in our church and my (only) role model, my family's divorce, my sister's abandonment of the situation for her own survival, body image issues, "who am I" yearnings, and just plain getting up in the morning. Trying to understand the nature of my depression, to separate, flag, and catalogue the new tears from the old ones that were backlogged by way of denial, naïveté, and cultural myopia, became my life for the next two years.

While I don't try to boast of my recovery being a miracle because it felt like anything but one, and I hated every second of it even though it all helped me see the two dangling carrots of illumination and perspective, I did recover and move on. I pictured myself getting lifted off the ground back there in Yosemite, being fed what paramedic hero John called the, "good trail mix with M&Ms," being put back together a là Humpty Dumpty, and being re-oriented to North.

What broke along with those bones and my spirit was my future in Northern California. My mom's new family had helped me to buy a restaurant/café to continue the catering I loved to do on the side. I used all the funds available to me to start up the business. I just ended a relationship with my college boyfriend after he tried to take a *step back* from our engagement to be married. I quit my university research job to pursue this café dream.

Talk about all my eggs. Now, I wonder if that basket I was stuffing wasn't found on the side of someone else's healthy, non-meandering life. I crutched along for a few months after the final surgery, and I couldn't walk normally for a year and a half total after my fall. This prognosis was given while I was still in the hospital, so I had to let go of the restaurant one month before its scheduled reopening under new ownership.

I began my search for what a childhood friend calls True North. After months of intensive physical therapy and some attempt at reinsertion into my social life, I got a lead and began to work for Americorps, our country's urban Peace Corps. I thought I had found it—working with middle school-aged kids by teaching life skills and art, and then leading them out into the cities and countrysides to help restore communities of

people and environmental landscapes. If I can also urbanize Peace Corps'
motto, Americorps was indeed the "toughest job I ever loved."

Still, it wasn't my niche.

While working my last semester in the Mission District of San Francisco, more of the bubbling that was triggered by Yosemite's experience
revealed itself. Eczema, a reasonably dormant skin disease that I had
inherited, began to eat me alive.

Within a few weeks of this unexpected surge from my family's history, I became a Petrie dish for all kinds of other skin ailments. I got
poison oak from hiking, and it stayed with me for an entire season.
Steroid shots made me worse, so I went into hiding. In this self-erected
cave (I had been too sick to work week after week), I got even sicker.
Compounding my disease and the poison oak, I got shingles in my eyes.
These strange, blistering lesions that are nerve-related, dozens of them
that spread within days from one eye to the next and down my face,
started to impair my vision. The dermatologist threw up the white flag
when he saw this latest.

Half-jokingly, he said, "My best advice to you would be to move to
an environment with a lot of fresh trade winds, humid air, and an ocean
for you to dip in every few days to get the healing effects of salt water. It
would do you good to get away and heal, too."

If surviving and healing from Yosemite was miracle #1, this makes
#2. I was at a night service for an alternative Christian church group. I
was hungry for some spiritual chicken soup, so I went in sunglasses and
a baseball cap. I didn't hear the message or the singing or even catch any
of the contagion those zealots were famous for. I was too itchy, painful,
and depressed to make the leap. Instead, I wallowed.

On my way out, an acquaintance called me on my anachronistic
"sunglasses at night." I briefly showed him my laundry list of skin woes,
and as I had expected, he asked if he could pray for me.

*Sure, why not. I was raised in a praying household. What have I got to
lose?*

My response was robotic; everyone in my circle of friends who were
God-fearing were praying for me as it was. After the prayer, he asked me

what I needed. I began my rehearsed litany of spiritual healing, more faith, and wisdom into this period of drought in my life.

"No," he interrupted, "I mean what do you need to help you get better physically?" I mentioned I needed to move to Hawai'i—a little sarcastic but again, what did I have to lose?—and since my sister took root there years earlier in part to escape our disintegrating family, I could live in her family's extra bedroom. I would be unemployed when I got there, so I needed some money to find a dermatologist who would treat me while I tried to de-stress enough to hold down a job and secure health insurance.

The next day, my neighbors who also attended that church walked over to our unit and gave me an envelope.

"We're not supposed to tell you where this came from, but Todd wanted to ask the church if they had any resources to help you. They don't know you, but they know us and we're your friends. This person says that you should use this to get well, and if there's any extra, give it to charity." My neighbors Andy and Maggie left in my hands an envelope with a check written out to me for one thousand dollars.

I moved to Hawai'i, and I found a private dermatologist to treat me because my health insurance had ended with my job in California. The miracle, if it can be marked, financially ended three months later on Oahu. I paid about a hundred dollars per weekly visit, and the doctor gave me meds and treatments and eventually did skin testing for allergies. In between the visits, I learned how to surf to get the salt water healing, I got a part-time teaching job at a private school, I held a waitressing job on Waikiki's South Shore so I could watch the surf (and get health insurance), and I waited. Through almost three seasons of the next year, I slowly learned to face people and myself again, and my skin forgave me and healed. The exactitude of this anonymous gift was that, as soon as my last visit to the doctor was over, I had spent $970.

Another thing happened while I was on my sabbatical from life on those islands. I began to dream about my *own* life. I had wondered, through the circuitous exoduses of broken bones, a torn family, a truncated romance, an ended Americorps appointment, and all the skin flare-ups, what my next step was. For several months, my eczema kept me from sleeping more than three hours a night. Yet, even those desperate, smashed-together minutes of trying to rest before I had to walk to the bus stop at 5:30 in the morning for my breakfast shift held enough tangible flash-frame dreams of moving to a place where I could have all the elements of what I valued most around me: my family and friends in California with whom I've always pictured myself growing old; the ocean that I now realized had always been courting me since the family trips to Santa Cruz; a population of people considered "less than" that I could invest in and work alongside; and finally, the chance to work, write, and be challenged among *my* native people, Californians.

When the dermatologist and allergist told me my success in the islands was limited because I was allergic to everything blooming there, and things bloom year round in tropical places, I bought my one-way ticket back to Berkeley.

While there, I looked feverishly into graduate school programs that had anything to do with Literature and/or Creative Writing. For me, it was easy to narrow down the hundreds of Lit. and Creative Writing programs to a few in Northern and a few in Southern California: I had to stay near fresh trade-winds, my family, community work, and the ocean.

(I admit I didn't stay long enough to excavate and polish any dusted-over gems in Hawai'i. That's why I never met more than handfuls at a time of rogue party-ers and spiritual surfers, all hilariously entertaining, all socialistically generous, all excellent sun and surf partners. *Surf's up sistah, let's go ride'em yah.* All stoned, 24/7. Not that I wouldn't have partaken of their generous, actual *Mau'i Wowie*, but these carefree days that slipped together into one long social hour happened for me in college, and by the time I was sick and in Paradise, those temptations had lost their sting. I just wanted to go to a café with a friend, journal and sip, occasionally share profound observations, raise the Questions, something I'd taken for granted as routine in Berkeley. Y'know, be "alone together." I was so intellectually emaciated by the time I got back to California that I convinced myself my island fever was just that, a hospital stay until I got well enough to digest the heated dogma and indomitable spirit of California, my homeland.)

I seriously looked at San Diego State University's Master of Fine Arts in Creative Writing program. I had to make the application deadline because I found the program last minute while trying to apply to other Northern California programs. I applied without visiting the area, and then I called a girlfriend who lived in the Mission Valley part of San Diego. I hadn't talked to her in years, but we grew up three houses down from each other, and our families were in the same *tropa*. She was a traveling nurse who made a three-month assignment last for almost a year by the time I made it down. She gushed about San Diego. She confided in me that she would make her last traveling assignment San Diego, and she would try to get a permanent position in the hospital she was already working in. San Diego was her dream home. I wasn't completely sold, mostly just curious, because even if we could have been cut from the same cloth, and we considered each other family, this woman and I led polar lives. After catching up, it appeared at the time that the only things we converged on were that we came from the same hometown, and we both loved the feel of the sand and the temperate weather. Everything else—from religious to social beliefs—we were each side of a coin.

During the months between my application to these programs and when I began to hear from them, I never made the time to visit San Diego. I had been to the area during one of my Spring Breaks in undergrad with my sorority sisters, but I spent most of that trip on top of a bar counter in Rosarito, Mexico or behind some guy's lips in Pacific Beach.

I got into the MFA program at San Diego State. The program that could have taken me in Northern California charged an amazing $20,000 a year in tuition alone. The day I received the we-want-you, I thought I should go to San Diego as soon as the weekend hit to see for myself.

I drove solo, more anxious with each green mile marker road sign. When they began to end city names with "Beach," I could feel my heart start. I had to do a double take when I saw there was actually a freeway that said "Beaches." I stayed with a couple of college friends I had found through e-mailing before the weekend, and they did their best to give me the tourist 4-1-1. Without knowing more than what my senses indulged in over one weekend of surfing on a borrowed board and getting martinis in downtown's Gaslamp District, I thought I should get a few yeas or nays because my instinct was on high alert, but I knew I was acting on too much passion, not enough logic.

ברּ

I've been living in San Diego for two years.

I amend that: I've been *alive* in San Diego for two years.

Speaking sun and water, I have been taking advantage of the recreation-heavy values of this city and of SDSU. Along with my literature classes and writing workshops, I get credit to take water sports classes such as surfing or wakeboarding. To most outsiders, I'm doing as the Romans do. I don't hold it against them; in fact, I'd rather be incognito with it, but their idea of R & R is part of what I need to make it through life at all. The pride people in San Diego take in nurturing their bodies as much as their minds and souls gives me the push I need to try and live as well as I can with my skin disease. I can't always get in the water when the eczema comes back and it's too painful, but any time I can surf or walk on the beach and remember where God has allowed me to tread, I can count nothing as giving me more peace.

I've been continuing to meet people who don't stretch what San Diego has to offer so much as they stretch me to try and see more and more of it. Circles of new family from the beach, my program, my jobs, and my church have adopted me. One of the women I met here says every person in our lives is around for a reason, a season, or for life. In the last year, while my head was turned I suppose, I met my "lifer." One of the professors at a local community college, a graduate and Golden Child from our MFA program, will be my husband in less than a month. Through his eleven years in San Diego, he has shown me where to go East of the I-5 every chance allowed, helping me to bridge old home to new home, just as he has from his New York origins to here. I have gone camping in deserts and done mountain peak-hiking in the snow an hour from the ocean. I have also become involved in teaching students in parts of San Diego that are less-connected with the Baywatch, affluent side most outsiders believe San Diegans to be. Working with ESL students in just one college of many, City College, I am immersed in more than twenty cultures and languages, including Filipino immigrants who could use a familiar look or word every now and again.

I still get sick with my eczema, and in fact this latest attack has lasted almost eight months—the longest and most arduous to date in my life—but I believe the indigenous levity of this atmosphere is what is making life bearable through these months, perpetuating an inimitable joy. It's a misconception we people have when we see the stereotypical bleachies and Coppertoned biceps tossing a volleyball around on one of the lined-up sand courts in South Mission. We mistake this lightness for shallowness, a lack of depth when it's more akin to buoyancy, and for me, hope. Wasn't it Oscar Wilde who said, "Life is too important to be taken seriously"?

When my psychologist told me that things bubble to the surface when we go through trauma such as illness, I walked away being afraid of the things that getting sick put in front of me, making me deal. Being in San Diego and having clean air, sand, and the ocean to nurture me by carving out vital breathing space for my condition, I join the ranks of 20-20 hindsighters. I see now that Being Sick makes only the things that matter float to the top. The high-spirited resilience of the mainstays that I value in my life—my future husband, my family, my community, the ocean, and personal growth—may be all the proof I need now that I'm not trying to build a home on someone else's jettisoned islands. These are my girders, my foundation, and the arrows towards my True North.

Most people in this country have the luxury to follow their hearts where it leads them. This is the American Dream. I concede: my mom did this, and the American Dream, although it took no prisoners, is hers. As for myself, I have had to follow my disease in order to simply live. It has taken me thirty years and a few trying seasons of island hopping, getting back on my feet over and over to accept the next challenge.

Today I stand in Ocean Beach, San Diego. If someone tries to sell me ignorant stereotypes and clichés—that San Diego is a tourist town, that it is homogeneous, unlivable, and uncultivated, that its beauty is only skin deep—I will invite them to stay two blocks from the water at our apartment, trade their clunky shoes in for a pair of flip flops, take them to see the tension we learn to live fruitfully in that is embodied by the Border itself, and I will tell them how my skin, indeed, has brought me here to find beauty. I will tell them that I am living in a place where there is enough ocean to keep me afloat in my own archipelago.

☙

Shortly after writing this, I started to lose footing on my island sanctuary. Little did I know this was not an end but only the beginning of the most challenging bout of eczema I would ever experience.

Education

Truths

Fred reminds me, through binary conveniences of phone calls and e-mails (rarely in person) that he's stuck in our state capital *workfighting* for the Supreme Court, *never for the money*, and that he envies me. My Berkeley-lensed writing has evolved into liberal, big-girl storytelling while his East Coast Ivy League philosophy papers took root in Law back here in Cali. Me and my writing-for-fun; him and his writing-for-fairness. So far, it's yielded him quenchless allegiance to justice and a nearly as unfillable two hundred thousand dollar necklace of debt on millstoned shoulders. In deference for our best friendship since high school, I listen to him set his truisms onto conveyer belts headed in my direction via phone lines.

Today, in between sighs coveting our high school suburbia days when our only two tensions were One, why my Biology group's miniature 3-D ecosystem of Antarctica—fimo clay penguins, harp seals, and whales inhabiting an active volcano molded by flour-dusted dough—got second place to his chromosomal Team XY's imaginary, cactus-arrayed, alien-creatured desert landscape in orbit, encapsulated in a tax-dollar-financed space shuttle (that they gleefully kick-rolled down a hill later) or Two, trying not to be labeled as Fresh Off the Boat Filipino as it seemed all of our naval town, immigrant parents pressured we might become if we failed to perform, Fred offered me another nugget.

> "Truths are like acorns, Ella," he said,
> falling to the ground with tapping noise,
> anonymous within days."

These small truths grow
at the feet of matured oak trees.

"The oaks—these—are the questions we have."
They've been growing, looming for hundreds of years,
the silent unanswered.

Soon the acorns, too,
will rise. Muscled, serpent arms will raise
knotted fists, shake us down from our
high-n-mightiness.

"The truths," he exhaled, "always grow
into more questions."

The questions, they crowd us
again and again.

I record his words, shut my journal. Both of us, now a few years and new worlds away from the detritus of rotting oaks that occupy abandoned municipal parks and conceal scattered identities on sidewalks of back then, back there. *How can a parent leave a child? Will I be able to survive where faces and tongues are not my own? Will I ever pay back this debt, make them proud? How far exactly can, "I'm not going to be like them" take me? Is it enough to know* **one** *friend believes?*

As Fred continues due diligence in his harvest of acorns, I walk, survey campus, suddenly sober, wide eyes taking in freshly landscaped fledgling trees, intimidating fists swinging low and at my face, still asking. We promise to actually come home, see each other during the holidays, visit our favorite English teacher together, and dust off, try to restore our homespun, private ecosystem while we race to remember the names of the two scientists who discovered we are all made of DNA.

First Time

First time I knew I was racist, the study break was over.

Three dormmates—all hyphenated Americans—deviate over cracked textbooks, twiddling pens.

"Do you laugh at racist jokes?"

"I know so many."

"So do I."

Pause.

We slink floorbound, huddled, whisper every bit of them: Italian, Jewish, Filipino. Those are us, so it's okay.

Subdued laughter. Continue.

Black, Chinese, Mexican, Pollack, Gay, Redneck, Retarded.

Split-sided yet culpable, tormented yet purged, we swallow, maintain silence.

A decade later when I understand I've lived a second-class citizenship my whole life, cue this memory. I've minoritized my own self.

Joke's on me.

A Couple of Cents About the Secrets
of Our Universe Concerning
the Quantum Theory
and Other Things

Stephen Hawking—omni-scientist—said this (hem and haw
at your own discretion):

If the universe is governed by rational laws,
which I believe it is, these laws shouldn't be an arbitrary patchwork,
but should fit together into some
unified framework.

This quest, I nod while at the search for this
Grand Unified Theory, *I want to be a part of finding it!*
Equations swimming (rather, treading after a large red-meat meal) between my ears,
I read on Quantum Theory, defined as such:
"space, though appearing to be empty,
is filled with virtual particle pairs that may
'fluctuate'
or appear for extremely short periods of time."

Fluctuate—appear, then
                                    disappear?
Space looking empty, but really   not?

After much contemplation, intense deliberation,
I call my circle of friends (i.e. the local Think Tank).
We convene to find these [invisible]   visible
                                    [invisible]   again things.

Quarks. Quarks.
Quarks? or Quirks in human behavior?
Ohhhh, one of us epiphanizes, *I know what these are—*
We, with bated breath, topple frontward—
they're simple pleasures.

SIMPLE PLEASURES we scream! Simple pleasures!
[invisible]
        visible   [invisible] again—simple pleasures:
finding a faded, fabric-softened dollar in your jeans pocket;
munching on your fast food fries and finding a stray onion ring,
or better yet, a curly fry
in the mix;
warm asphalt on bare feet;
your face on a freshly flipped, cold pillow;
finding a personal letter sandwiched by all the bills
        (phone, maxed out card, insurance, magazine renewal, car payment,
        jury duty, via air mail letter from dad in the Philippines,
        another maxed out card, overdue library books);
a smooth street, a glassy wave, virgin snow to board down
(and no one to watch you yell your tonsils raw!);
free refills
free gift with purchase
free time on a parking meter
free *anything*;
being a good driving Samaritan, then getting
the courtesy wave;
[AOL voice] *You've got mail*;
good skin, good hair, good keep-away-from-donuts day;
any Brady Bunch episode, but especially the Grand Canyon Series or
the Hawai'i Trilogy *[insert "taboo" sampling here]*;
turning on the radio to hear your best karaoke-the-hell-out-of-it song;
getting home to see the <blink> <blink> <blink>
of answering machine love;
ice screeeaam cakes;
parking spaces downtown;
killing that itch;
not to forget the locking eyes with *him*, that all over bear hug
from a plucky kid who doesn't know
(or care) about public image.

That's it! we high-fiving, *we've figured out the secrets to our Universe!*
This chaotic soup, we've got the recipe!

Later that morning (because we labored
into the wee hours) I pick up my book. Still buzzing,
and in spite of our liberating discovery, I read on.
Then I see, on page 119, ole Albert E.:

The harmony of natural law...reveals an intelligence of such superiority that,
compared with it all, all the systematic thinking and acting of human beings
is an utterly
                    insignificant
                                        reflection.

Utterly insignificant? Human beings?

What does Einstein know anyway?
I bet he's never found an onion ring in his fries.

Foreplay

What day's "Saturday Night Live" on? How long is "Sixty Minutes"? What year did the War of 1812 happen? Who's buried in Grant's tomb? Did you know there are three "l"s in the word "gullible?" Is there raw fish in your pocket, or are you just happy sashimi? What are the sexiest animals on a farm? Brown chicken, brown cowwww. If you're walking down the street, and all the wheels fall off your canoe, how many elephants would it take to cover up your pancake? An orange because motorcycles have four doors. D'wanna study together?

Ahh, joyful, awkward, college-virgin foreplay.

The Belle Curve

Except for my monomaniacal fixation on adorning my red and white Apache-embroidered varsity letterman jacket with patches of tennis rackets and badminton shuttlecocks, I could have been an entrepreneur in my teens. On report card day, my parents paid my sister and me five dollars for each A we earned, three dollars for each B, and a buck for each C. I didn't keep an eagle eye on the money reward at the end of each quarter, but having a small chunk of spending money to take to the mall was a nice bonus.

Don't get me wrong. I was definitely greedy and wanted to go to the next Depeche Mode or Madonna concert at the Oakland Coliseum as bad as the next 80s teen, but in the area of grades, money was no longer an external motivator for me. By the time I was in high school, I was culturally programmed to believe the only acceptable grades were straight As. The family tradition, in every letter to relatives in the Philippines, at every holiday *tropa* party (or in line at Safeway talking to any stranger who happened to be Filipino as well) of saying, "My daughter has always been a straight-A student. She's going to college to be a doctor. And how are your children doing in school?" fanned this flame. [*Cut to me: picking lint off of my letterman, wondering where to sew the final shuttlecock when Coach Russell handed them out end of the season.*] Fortunately, it was a simple equation to reach these grades. In the Honors classes where my best friends and I were always in "healthy competition" for top dog (English, History, Calculus, Biology) I memorized plots, characters, World War timelines, equations, and organelle functions thanks to Cliffs Notes and index cards. I needed to score 100% (preferably better) on any assignment. Extra credit was never *extra*; it was obligatory. In classes that were more "shop" than college prep (Government, Economics, Physical Education), earning 93% sufficed. (90-92% was an A–…why even risk my parents noticing and possibly having a "talk" about slipping grades?).

This system served my parents' pride and apparently the whole of the Philippine Islands' reputation well. For me, it was one quiet assurance that I could control a part of who I was and how others perceived me. With my bank of $30 in my wallet at report card time, I knew I was one of the smartest students in high school. I also knew my parents were making sure our cousins' parents and their cousins' neighbors' supermarket acquaintances knew that the "deCastro daughter" was a top student.

Having this adulation ameliorated many less-than-popular high school realities, including that I had to ask the new guy (who we named "River Phoenix" because we couldn't remember his name) in our English class to go to the prom with me because I wasn't asked by anyone else, that my first boyfriend in high school was for only a month until his rebound with me bounded him back to his three year girlfriend (a fresh hickey from her on his neck sealed this fate, and I never got that first kiss), that I could never tease my bangs or perm my waist-length hair in just the right way like the most popular, beautiful girls, that the high points of my week were seeing if I could hone my overhead clears and cross-court short smashes to challenge Carolyn to be the number two seed in Singles Badminton. Even though we lived in a cultural vacuum, having an impressive GPA balanced out my social and romantic inexperience. If excellent grades = responsible person = good heart = attractive personality, it all made me feel above-average, even successful. Why would I even suspect that as soon as I sat down in my first lecture class on the first day at college, this predictable system of merit would become obsolete?

&

At UC Berkeley (where no one wore their costly, personalized letterman jackets by the way, unless it was tie-dyed) science and math classes were largely graded based on the Bell Curve. It was a system of grading based on frequency distribution of scores on a test or assignment. The shape of this distribution curve was like a bell, with the top of the bell being the average score, a C grade on a test or assignment. At either ends of the curve, a small number of A grades as well as F grades were slotted. The professor of the class would decide what percentage of the class members could compete for and receive each letter grade. Usually, at the end of the semester, this is how the final class grades were also decided.

For example, in our Chemistry 1A class that I took during the first year at Cal, there were about 1,100 students. When we took our midterm exam, students were given a percentage of how much of the exam we answered correctly, from 0–100%. Instead of the traditional letter to percentage correlation where 90–100% = A, 80–89% = B, etc., the Bell Curve took whatever score was the highest, and a certain number of students who scored around that score received the A grade. Most students received scores from 50–70% on the midterms. Normally, this would mean those students got Cs, Ds, and Fs. But, with the Bell Curve, if the highest grade in the class was only an 80%, say, then a student with a 50% would not get an F grade but a C because the student with the 80% would receive the A and set the curve. This could be a good thing for the many students trying to pass a really difficult class because it elevates their grades. (But, no matter how beneficial the curve may be to a student's grade, getting a D curved to a B still only means the student's knowledge of the class material is a D.)

Nevertheless, at Cal, this was usually not the case. If the Law of Large Numbers proves true, in a class of 1,100 students taking a Chemistry or Calculus class—and all of the students came from high schools where apparently they were salutatorian or valedictorian of their graduating class (as was my entire dorm floor except for one roommate who failed out the second semester)—that meant that even if most students would have scored in the "average" range, the highest score on a midterm might as well have been perfect because there also always seemed to be a genius registered in any given science or math class. In my Chem class, there happened to be at least three geniuses (excuse me, "geniusi"—plural, thank you) who scored near-perfect scores, so the curve didn't elevate my 55% test score enough to make a difference. To add insult to injury, the curve and the professor set the limit on how many people could get certain letter grades. If the top 1% could get A grades, and the next 5% Bs, that meant after a certain number of students earned their Bs, even if there was a student with a score in the 80% range, if there wasn't any more room in the B grading category, that student was lumped in the largest grouping, the Cs.

℃

For the first half of my undergrad years, I had to endure the shock and grieving stages of losing the hometown staples of my identity: Filipinos as far as the almond-shaped eye could see, rice with every meal (including breakfast eggs), and attainable good grades. Having been torn from Vallejo's womb, I had to learn so many new things. I had to learn that adults in Berkeley did not speak to me in Tagalog. I hadn't realized that I understood my family's language fluently until I stopped hearing the tribal, "bubbling pot"-like sounds on campus (I always assumed, since our parents trained us to reply in English to avoid "fob" accents and being typecast as ignorant immigrants, I didn't know the language). Also, there apparently were other Asian American people groups besides Filipino Americans because even though we looked similar, every Asian I passed was speaking an unrecognizable dialect beyond our 100-plus regional tongues. Later, I learned Asians also spoke Korean, Mandarin, Japanese, Taiwanese, even Laotian.

When I searched out the other Filipinos at Cal, the Filipino circles hanging out on campus that I assumed would gather me into the fold did the opposite. They interacted as if they were their own *tropa* of family members hanging out in someone's garage party—laughing, spouting off in Taglish (same idea as Spanglish, Taglish = Tagalog-English, the slang language of our 1st generation), overacting drunk even though their cups had Coke in 'em. Instead of leaving space in the circle for me to "busta move," I was overtly unwelcomed. During the first months of Pilipino American Association (PAA) club meetings, I tried to mill in with the

200 or so members in the lecture hall, listening for an entry into any clique's conversation. No one greeted me, asked if I knew Auntie So and So, or told me they heard I was a "top student" from their mom while visiting home for the weekend.

(At first, I thought this behavior highly uncharacteristic of Filipinos because in Vallejo, we just belonged, no question about it. Our fathers worked at Mare Island Naval Shipyard, we lived on the same block with each other since elementary school, and we went to the same regional festivals and parades. Soon though, I could see how this segregationist behavior was also a "normal" Filipino occurrence. Being a people who kept getting territory taken from them, we became paranoid and territorial in return. A popular metaphor is that Filipinos are crabs in a bucket. We all live together fine, sharing what little resources we have in that bucket. But when we see one crab climbing on top of everyone else, trying to get a leg—or claw—up and over the bucket and out into the free world, the rest of us pull that crab back into the bucket. Maybe I could have earned these peoples' trust if I persisted in going to the meetings. Or they just didn't have room for me in their bucket.)

This new world forced me to live as if I was an individual. My family and culture no longer engulfed me, informing me of who I was, providing me with instant friends and extended family, or determining that I was a successful student and young woman. For the first time, I had to earn my grades, and by direct implication, my identity *for* myself and *by* myself.

I stopped looking for others that looked like me and began joining groups that felt and (re)acted like me. Since my dorm roommate was interested in joining a Christian club, I decided since I was raised in a religious home, I should, too. When we outgrew the dorm, we both pledged a sorority. We had no idea what being in the Greek system meant, having forgone Sorority Rush where we could have visited each of the 17 sororities on campus and been given a bird's eye glimpse into what we were actually committing to. I bumped into a woman from Vallejo who was older than me, and she said I should bring my roommates and visit her sorority for a casual dinner. We loved the three-story mansion, saw the rooms were larger than our dorm room and cost significantly less than dorm fees, and when we were asked back again and formally invited to "pledge," we were ecstatic.

All this means in everyday language is that there was no chance for someone as distracted as me by all the brilliant-minded, experimental, double-mocha-soaked, dynamic, hemp-woven, activist, green, multi-ethnic and fraternity/sorority culture of Berkeley, U.S.A. from doing homework, studying, or even plain concentrating to rise above that bell curve and coast down towards one of my "normal" high school grades. I was either having awkward social hour with all the hundreds of other students lumped on the hill of Average Grades or sliding on my belly, face down, towards the D and F tail of the bell.

∽

This is a composite daily log of my daily jog up and down the Belle Curve during my undergraduate years at UC Berkeley. It is the same curve as the original Bell, but this is based on a young woman's ability to feel, live, and most critically, be perceived—or scored—according to tests aimed at determining one's academic, worldly, spiritual, and even physical worth, or minced words aside, one's "prettiness."

Tuesday

After InterVarsity Christian Fellowship (IVCF) Large Group meeting, Maggie walked back up the hill to the sorority house to study, and I strolled a few blocks from First Presbyterian Church to Raleigh's Pub for glass night. I motioned to my Big Sis in the sorority, Tilda, already inside the bar behind the glass window separating us, and another sister at the table walked out to greet me, slip me Tilda's ID. I flashed her real, my fake ID at the bouncer (my Big Sis is a Chinese American, but since we "Orientals" all look the same—slanted eyes, long black hair, flat noses, my fake identity that day was Chinese girl from Rowland Heights, California). When I turned 21 and could use my own ID, I paid it forward to the next "Asian Invasion" sorority girl infiltrating pubs for beer glass night, adding to the "around the world" feel inside the bar, not just inside the souvenir pint glass imprinted with the import beer logo of the week.

We sat around the wood-stained table, pint glasses bouncing light across the bar, reflecting the Greek house "uniforms" all around us: Cal baseball caps and backwards visors, intramural championship or football game fundraiser tees, individual Greek letters on cotton shirts and tank tops across puffed out chests (both sexes), a few blue and gold rugby shirts flanked by signature blue and white striped Adidas soccer slippers. The subtle, swishing sound of shuffleboard-cushioned beer gulps and high fives. There was the cracking clacking rolling sinking rumble of pool balls from chalked stick to pocket. Sometimes, I had the honor of being the "mixed doubles" partner for Shaun. He, a pool shark in standard frat-boy uniform while ironically very anti-Greek (yet still dating me, but according to him, our House did not fit the stereotypical stuck-up, homogeneous "top houses" because our 100-member sorority population was as ethnically and socioeconomically diverse as the college campus). I smiled, pointing my pool stick in the direction and angle he instructed me, trying to look cute while making the shot (I seemed to be the most dexterous at it with a couple of pints in me—not drunk yet, but brain-buzzed, on my way).

It took several months of weekly Tuesday glass night visits for me to finally acquire the taste for beer, virgin taste buds learning the darker the beer the better (I drank beer only once in high school at a Model United Nations conference field trip, from a generic white can with black letters, B-E-E-R across it). Until the point I could drink and enjoy the Around the World beer and rightfully earn the "Around the World" t-shirt one could only attain after getting a "passport" stamped for each of the 30 or so beers on the membership card, whoever was sitting next to me basically got himself, after my few pained gulps, a free beer for graciously draining the glass I wanted to take back to the House.

There was even San Miguel from the Philippines for a short while until they stopped including it on the newer cards. It's an okay beer but not my favorite. The most exciting part of drinking this beer was having it for the first time in the Philippines with cousins at a dance club in 1991. After just having one, I was a stage-dancing idiot, already conspicuous because I was an *Americana* and also happened to be *matangkad,* so "tall" for a woman at 5'3". Later, I learned that San Miguel export laws guaranteed the alcohol content level in the beers countries like the U.S. would sell, but in the P.I., there were no such laws. So, one bottle of San Miguel could have the usual one beer's worth of alcohol in it while the next one could have four times the alcohol content!

I would remember this trivia the next time I was in the Philippines on a missions trip. During our debrief on a small island, Boracay, that we flew a smaller plane to, our group shared a generous meal of minutes-fresh crabs, salted fish over rice, and beer. After the work we did earlier running Vacation Bible School for the dozens of kids in a squatter area near Metro Manila and sharing a one bedroom apartment between five college students, we needed a small vacation ourselves to process the abject poverty and anomalous unmediated, childlike joy we were shocked to find in the midst of it. I was in need of a beer, or ten (my commitment to Glass Night in Berkeley tempered my drinking threshold, often requiring me to drink several beers and/or half a dozen mixed drinks at other bars or parties in order to simply get buzzed).

As vulnerable as I was from my first international missions experience, I didn't want my dual personality to foam over onto these respectable Christian friends' laps. So, I nursed two beers for the whole night. As a bonus for trying (at last) not to fill my status-quo-conflicted, hypocritical identity, my second beer had the roll-of-the-dice four beers' worth alcohol content. Thanks also to the heat and humidity, I was giddily drunk by the time we found a place to dance the night away. If only I could find my standard "boy toy" chaser who would walk me home and kiss me goodnight on the steps of the sorority house (or in one of the Suitor's rooms*), the mission trip "debrief" would have been complete.

---

* When our sorority was built at the turn of the 20th century, a Suitor's room was the only place a male was allowed to talk to/spend time with a Sister. Built in the common area of the mansion, these two small sitting rooms came to serve more as markers of antiquity than utility. Since men were now allowed in other parts of the house in the 90s (except in bedrooms after 10 p.m.), we reserved the Suitor's rooms for guests or to study.

Wednesday

Hump day, or pretend dry hump day (after a few close calls, I was still a member of the Virgin's Club, and proud of it—not in a peacock way, more in the closet sort of way). Two or three of us (whoever didn't have a midterm or paper the next day) would get in line at Blake's for the explosive underground dance party. Blake's is a dinner place, a mixed-drink bar with shot specials and free popcorn after Cal game days, and a well-known venue for live jazz. Once a week, the owners pre-empted their regular schedule to pay a local DJ to make people dance. Dancing meant carte blanche for me; something in my Flip bloodlines proved I could adapt to the latest moves at will, and 70s and 80s music triggered a hyper-verve-ness I couldn't explain with words. I danced with my girl-friends, alone, or with any guy confident enough not to expect me to talk or walk with him after. These nights, I didn't have to drink a drop of anything (although I did take sips of friends' drinks because I was truly thirsty.) It was, however, another indulgence for me.

Since DJs are their own marketing machines, the guy who spun records on these nights brought his entourage to pack the dance floor. Berkeley locals infused with a healthy variety from other drinking-age groups such as Division One athletes, Greek brothers and sisters, and Co-op residents kept Telegraph Avenue on the Southside of campus abuzz all hours of the day (seemed the engineers and pre-med studs stayed on Northside—probably a smart move to avoid temptation). Blake's patronage was usually a reflection of this diverse population. However, what was distinctive about this night every week is that, as the reputa-tion of the music style grew—funk, some groove, plenty of old school rap, hip hop once in a while—this drew a crowd that included a large community of Black men. These Black men were not accompanied by Black women, though. Some came to enjoy the vibe, some each other's company, some the liquor, and some the dance company of undergradu-ate women eagerly taking study breaks. Every week, I could count on meeting a generous handful of these non-locals (and a few white men who acted and believed they were Black), and at least one of them would feed my ego with conflicted but craved attention.

"Wow—you're so different looking," one would say as he grabbed my hand on the dance floor. I'd smile and keep dancing, unthreatened. As he insisted we dance together for several songs spread out during the night, I eventually heard the Label.

"You're so pretty—in a way that's so *exotic*." Sometimes he even added, "Has anyone ever called you that?"

Now, I can't say I know what or who to blame for that derogatory term, *exotic*. I think it might have begun as a genuine adjective for Asian women by people who were innocently taken by the "look" of a woman from Asia: foreign, brought from elsewhere, not native. Eventually, of course, the term was deemed prejudiced because Asians could be even more native to the U.S. than the non-Asian person exclaiming our "foreign" look (like I was—born and raised in Northern California). It also suggests we're like imported fruit or furniture, objects. Nope. Nevertheless, when I heard it from these men on these Wednesday nights, I often trusted they meant it as a compliment, not a premeditated reversal of feminism. I also simply adored being adored.

On the flip side, being called "exotic" did, I must say, sometimes feel like a reality reminder that my allure was no more than superficial, even a caricature of the *me love you long tine* and *me so horny* Asian honey to many other men I'd met at other bars or walking down the street minding my own. All in all, I consciously accepted the compliment. Even as I knew—from all my feminist-tinged Teaching Assistants, Professors, classmates, and an assortment of naked lesbian Berkeleyans protesting for their rights—just how righteously angry I needed to be at men who objectify Asian women this way, I liked being called this kind of pretty. I told myself attention was attention, and Man-tention? All the more fulfilling.

Strangely, as much of a mini-celebrity as me and my minority girlfriends were on those nights, I never let the men I met from these nights walk me home. Clearly high on the adrenalin of nonstop dancing, I was dead sober, and Someone Up There must have helped me take these infrequent moments of lucidity serious enough to inject self-confidence into me. I would walk home with my girlfriends, undaunted and untempted, somehow slaked by the *exotic* remarks. I enjoyed their dark eyes groove and gyrate up and down my petite, brown frame. Maybe because they seemed to overlook my flat-chested demise and instead celebrated a disproportionately fuller butt, framing large, dense Asian calves. To these men, the darker and kinkier the sweat made my hair, the better. The less contained I got, the more they unraveled in glorifying me, and the more I could be fully myself, setting a standard on the dance floor that other Greek, perfect, lofty, white, blond, buxom counterparts would never (want nor be able to) attain.

I made a few solid friends there, some I felt I could trust. One of them was a hilarious local young man who chose not to finish college and instead work at the Boys Club, mentoring Black boys around the East Bay whose life circumstances mirrored those he experienced. Bob was 6'5", thin, with profoundly warm, brown eyes, enviously long and curly lashes, a welcoming smile (with a touch of devil in one corner), an unwrinkled, unpierced, unblemished complexion: the kind of handsome guy whose face probably looked exactly the same when he was a first grader. Bob danced with me and all my girlfriends whenever he saw us, sometimes sharing his long island iced tea with me, then going off to flirt at will. He never stood in line, never paid the $5 cover, and was never without company. Guys and girls respected him and loved him. When we saw him walking around Telegraph or on campus (this town raised him, so he knew more than any transient college student would ever know), we called out his name and made efforts to shake his hand or kiss each other on the cheek. Of the many, many months Blake's hosted this weekly, gritty dance club, Bob had perfect attendance. It would follow then, that eventually, as I sipped more of his long island each passing dance, I eventually "asked" him to walk me home.

At this point, I had been what my sorority girlfriends and I termed, a "kissing hoe." I had my first no-strings kiss at after a fraternity-sorority exchange when I asked a pledge from the fraternity to walk me home. He reached over and kissed me, and then he left and never called. I saw him at parties after that, but there was no weirdness. It was par for the course. After I realized I had a knack for this kiss-n-who-cares "hobby," I started to record the interludes in my journal. I numbered the guy, listed his name and if he was in a fraternity, described what he looked like, what we chatted about or songs we danced to, what drinks he bought or mixed for me, his major and year, and anything else that was interesting. At the end of each brief bullet-point bio, I scored the kissability of each guy, from 1–10. I had enough research to compile and analyze that the average kissing ability for the guys my lips "bumped" into was a "7." Not bad (even if it does translate to a C on a standard grading system, on my curve, it was closer to a B+ based on lip tingles and heightened hormones). Sadly, I did kiss a "1" on this scale. He was the trumpet player for a jazz band that I danced to at a co-op party. Maybe I had inflated hopes because he played the trumpet flawlessly (any artist made me swoon) although saying it felt like I was kissing the tongue of a rain-soaked boot isn't good on any account.

(In case you're wondering what stats a "kissing hoe" holds: after a couple of years, I stopped recording when I hit 50 guys and saw that sometimes I didn't even know a guy's name, maybe just what he was wearing, if his arms had muscles, and of course, what his kissing score was. I stopped recording, but it took me a couple more years to stop accruing test subjects and data.)

When Bob walked me home, everyone was awake, some drunk, some studying. A few sisters recognized Bob from bars and campus, gave him hugs, welcomed him. We walked to the TV room to snuggle, eventually lie down and spoon. I wasn't sure I should kiss Bob because I actually liked him as a person and wanted to keep talking to him after that night. I didn't want to have a vibe-less rapport in order to mask that we "hooked up" and had to be noncommittal adults about it. When the last sister left the TV room to go to sleep, and Bob brushed his full bottom lip against my smaller but also full bottom lip, I gave in. Hours and hours later, watching Bob walk down the hill in the chill of 3 a.m., I knew I would record him as my perfect, and only "10." On this test, he set the curve, that genius.

I didn't know what to do with Bob because he wasn't shallow enough to follow any fraternity and sorority social hook-up "fratiquette." He began to visit me, read me eloquent poems, and dream out loud about how he wanted to start his own nonprofit youth center to help tutor and coach young Black boys in academics, basketball, football, and by extension, both sides of the same coin: success, survival. I felt lame because I used this motivated, deep, and awesome human being for entertainment. He was my exotic toy for the night, and though I didn't use the label outright, I still felt like I exploited him. Eventually, he caught my drift and stopped trying to open up to me. For the remainder of that season, we waved at each other across Blake's as we danced with other partners.

℣

To complicate the innocuous bell curve, in 1994 a nationally heralded book was published called *The Bell Curve, Intelligence and Class Structure in American Life*. The entire campus was chattering about its many claims regarding IQ testing and how it could predict not just intelligence, but social and economic behaviors. In other words, a person with a low IQ test would be more likely to end up on welfare, committing crimes, or even having a child out of wedlock than another who scored higher on the test. As soon as it was widely praised as groundbreaking research, it was protested in true Cal fashion by an impressive sampling of undergrads, professors, and prestigious researchers in their fields.

One of the main arguments against the book was that it promotes scientific racism because it suggests, among other claims, that IQ is inherited and immutable and a better indicator of an individual's future success than the person's socioeconomic status. It then analyzes data and leads readers to infer that since Black Americans, on this distribution curve, score lower than White Americans in IQ, it is therefore more likely that Blacks would travel down the road towards welfare…you get the picture…than Whites. In one instance, the authors actually suggest that Black women be severed from receiving welfare because they had been using the program as a sanction to have more children—children who will also, statistically and inevitably, score lower on the IQ test than their white counterparts.

Equally outraged and inquisitive about how I would interpret this book, and more importantly, where Asian Americans would settle on this curve, I asked for a copy of the almost 1,000 page tome from my friends. Finding the book at Costco, two friends dropped off copies within days. I realized I could barely carry my school textbooks to and from class, so these books ended up filling out a corner of my closet. I did slide one of them open to skim for any data or tables with clear explanations of where "my" kind of people hung on this bell, but I managed to fail even this simple test of following through on a thought.

The Real reason I didn't read the book may be rooted in fear. What if there's some truth to this scientific racism? Where does that leave me? Where does that leave Bob and the young Black boys he mentors? Where does that leave his dreams?

Thursday

Freshman dorm roommates and now Pledge Sisters, Maggie and I walked to College Avenue to a weekly Bible Study named "Friendship Circles." Goal: learn how to represent Jesus to our friends on campus in ways that were inclusive, authentic, and eventually invitational. One member, Grace, was brokenhearted before she reached Jess' condo. We put aside our study to listen to her tell us her parents announced they were divorcing, how shocked she and her brother were, and that she was devastated and depressed. We lay hands on her and prayed what we should have prayed—comfort, peace "that passes understanding," a deeper trust in God's overall plan for her family. She wept openly. I cried silently, a taste in my mouth of my parents' divorce announced just months earlier. Her tears sang a familiar, mournful dirge in my ears because as a Chinese-American, she was also part of an overachieving Asian-American family; without having to ask, I knew how crushing this could be for everything Grace and her family built to uphold the reputation of Model Minority.

The noise in my head thrashed around like wrecking balls in mid-demolition. Buildings that once stood, tremor-proof, razed instantly into desert sand. There was Grace—newly-obliterated, next to me—still oblivious, wondering when the smoke would finally clear. We might have sung some worship songs. We might have moved on to study the topic of taking our faith and the gospel into one-on-one relationships where Jesus connected most profoundly with people.

After ending the study with general prayer for our friends and any pressing academic needs, Maggie walked back home to study, and I walked one street down to meet straggling Sisters after the official dinner exchange with Lambda Chi fraternity—basically a mirror-image of our ethnic make-up and therefore also not a "top house." I had one-half cup of alleged rum and coke, later to find it was also spiked with Everclear—illegal 198 proof flavorless, colorless alcohol that fraternities made "quick" Nevada runs for. Michelle and I ended up in one of the fraternity bedrooms, spilling our toxic cocktail on someone's Mac keyboard. A second later, a couple of brothers came upstairs to see us rolling around on the floor, giggling and wrassling while also wondering why we were so inexplicably effed up over one drink. True, we enjoyed social drinking, but we were actually Not the most precarious, unpredictable, party-favor-like socialites in the house. We were more like the cute Asian girls that some guys enthusiastically watched dance with rehearsed, intentional dance routines (even rhythm) at social exchanges (Michelle was all exoticism in one: half Korean, half Black).

The other sisters had to carry us between their shoulders, dragging our incompetent legs and arms into our beds. I don't know how Michelle fared that night, but it was the night I added Everclear to my long list of allergies. I was projectile-vomiting into a plastic garbage can one sister held two feet away while another sister wondered out loud if she should call paramedics. When the last drop of poison was exorcised, I was left to dry heave on my own.

In the shared bathroom, I overheard the adjoining room recapping their night. Even though Patricia was at the same post-dinner exchange party I was at, I don't remember seeing her. In any case, the night apparently yielded an oral tale for prosperity: rolling Patricia up in a Persian area rug in their common room, four Lambda Chi's picked up the passed out burrito (heavy on the ever-sauce) and carried her up one street to hand-deliver her to our family room carpet.

Friday, Saturday, Sunday

I asked and received the official answer to my freshman question, "Is being in a fraternity like the movie *Animal House?*" Big sister Tilda got us two seats on a 'bago, as in Winnebago, rented by one of the Theta Chi's brother's father's credit card. Thus began our yearly exodus to the Cal vs. USC or Cal vs. UCLA football games—they rotated being in Southern Cali. Plastic red Solo cups in hand, innocent flirting and joking, everyone in sun visors that read "Go Bears" or "Cal" on them. Mine, one of my many, many armfuls of pro-AOPi and pro-Cal initiation gifts from my appointed Big Sister. An expert puffy painter with a steady hand to recreate the unofficial "sorority girl" curlicue font, Tilda handily inscribed Golden bear paws around "AOII" and "Roll On You Bears!" with yellow and white bubble letters on plastic blue—a cheerleader-y sight to behold.

The Winnebago was spacious, fresh, organized, a sign that it was not ours, so we better take care of it. By the time we cruised down Interstate 5 south and reached Fraternity Row at USC, the toilet was clogged (no more freshness), the keg was tapped, and the chumminess of having to squish shoulder to shoulder a sweaty drudgery. Big Sis Tilda had fended off two advances from ever-confident, drinking bros. I was yet a fresh Pledgling, so perhaps an unsaid rule was honored to keep their paws off me (probably until/unless I initiated the beer goggling exchange.)

Although these were the years our Pac 10 football team went to a Bowl game each postseason, we probably lost the SC game. No matter, to soothe our loss, the 'bago was taken to Tijuana. One of the best decisions for me was to stay this side of the border, making new friends with other undergrads whose fraternity house we borrowed sleeping bag floorspace in. When we left southern California several hours after our EDT, the debunked toilet also had a mangled door with a hole the size of a meathead's, well, head. Sticky cushions, floors, windows, and seats unloaded us back onto the fraternity steps on Durant Street. Tilda and I walked the block home, straight into the communal shower room, exhausted, cramped, with puffy eyes and livers.

Sunday Night

Patricia, Sonya, Michelle and I walked down Prospect Avenue to the end of the block, down another half block to Newman's Catholic Church for the contemporary 10 p.m. service. There was no lighting save for a small collection of votives burning to signify small and large prayer needs by desperate college students and local Berkeley parishioners. Following a stereotypically short liturgy (Catholics are champions of one hour masses, down to the minute, unlike the Black Seventh-Day Adventist church I was raised in) and right before Catholics were invited to take Communion, a list of prayers was said out loud by anyone in the congregation trusting enough to publicize their needs—for AIDS, for the gay community to feel loved (Newman ordained gay priests and had a support group for gays), for the environment, for someone's sick grandfather in Massachusetts, for a family who lost their daughter to cancer.

The next prayers were labeled "unsaid" and the priest appropriated thirty seconds of silence for us to think in the direction of God. My "unsaids" were to find a way to stay focused to study for upcoming midterms, to finish the Shakespeare paper, to be able to be pissed off at my mom for having the affair *without* having another nervous breakdown—and this time, avoid a crisis of faith—to know my sister was doing okay in Hawai'i since we hardly spoke to each other, to figure out how to extend that "alive" feeling when singing worship songs at Large Group—where everything's possible and looking Up is really a natural posture—beyond those first 25 minutes every Tuesday night before the teaching.

Quieted from the overload weekend, even solemn for a bit, we bumped into Bob walking home, him on his way from getting a slice of pepperoni to visit a friend taking a study break in a nearby apartment. We said we'd be in touch.

Monday

After going to lecture classes and sitting and sifting through seas of hundreds of faces per class, all taking notes, I was trying not to fidget in my seat while in awe that the novel I was perpetually behind in was written by the woman at the bottom of the stadium lecturing her deep, novelistic secrets at us. Then, I walked to the Northeast side of campus to take my one Calculus class (make-up class—I got a C⁻ the first semester even with daily tutoring, study groups and extra credit). I paused while walking through the parking lot next to Physical Sciences Lab (PSL). I remember entering Cal a Biology major and taking Chemistry 1A here. The ginormous book I was muscling to class three days a week was bursting with elementary and brilliant chemistry wisdom (almost a thousand pages), written by the small-framed East Asian professor lecturing in front of a lab table and large screen where he laser-pointed at covalent bonds. In the same auditorium-sized lecture hall, Professor Filippenko taught us the A, B, Comets of Astronomy 10. He was animated, *filipp*-ing out about dark matter and the microwave wall in outer space. We had to stargaze (beer and wine optional but highly recommended) on top of the tallest building on campus.

These classes were at least 1,100 seats (sometimes, there were 1,400 students, so some of us watched the professor lecture on TV in an overflow room a few buildings down). All the seats were full there, in the PSL, and I looked forward to seeing these professors getting out of their fuel-efficient cars, possibly parked in the adjacent Nobel Laureate parking lot. You had to have your "NL" parking permit to park in one of the 8 or 10 spots. Gawd, dare to dream.

After classes, I met Patricia at the Bear's Lair or on the steps of Sproul Hall. We went to the gym to wait for the newest gadget, the Stairmaster—45 minute wait—so I worked on upper body and crunches. As an inexpensive and nonfattening reward, we got the usual small chocolate and vanilla swirl yogurt at Yogurt Park, walking and licking all the way home. Later that night, we walked back down the hill to Strada Café for a bianca mocha. Thinking we studied better in groups and far away from the large-screen TV in the TV room and equally far away from our third-story beds, we reconfigured the sorority house Suitor's room to be study-ready. The ritual continued as we opened books and notebooks and started up the small Mac computer everyone had where the screen was only maybe 10 inches wide and only typed green letters in one font [hear the dot-matrix printer, line by line, chugging down the page].

Sonya didn't like coffee tastes, so she made herself a three-tea-bag strong hot tea and did jumping jacks to wake up. Michelle ate M & Ms and other chocolate-based goods (no coffee for her either). Patricia started to write her essays on Ethnic Studies, or sometimes she was in the TV room watching a required film for Film class. Thirteen minutes later, we started gossiping about who kissed who and who was going to try and crash what "top house" exchange the next weekend. Who had a new fake ID to try in San Francisco when we went to the Triangle and bar-hopped. What co-op party was also happening (it was good to hit up those friends' social options now and again). Did anyone see what's his nickname (Mexico Mike, Demi-God, etc.) at the Bear's Lair for happy hour Friday afternoon? Fade to black with scene of us falling asleep in the Suitor's room, all the lights on, the tea still steeping, the Bianca mocha corroding my molars, guaranteeing five fillings the next dentist visit.

(It may be too late to say this and reverse the stereotype I've affirmed by my own choices, but let me please clarify that my nonchalant academic behavior in the Greek system is not typical of fraternities and sororities. The Greek system—in its defense—really does place a high value on academics. In fact, Greek GPAs were and are always higher than the university GPA average. My GPA was *not* above the university average, by the way, nor was it at the Greek system average. I used to say that, together with another sister's GPA, we had a 4.0.)

Next Tuesday

Sonya, Michelle, and me, hitting the bottom of the curb, and curve, got our scruples together and decided to enlist in the Army to help give us direction, pay for college, and offer us purpose. It was an impulse that was anything but easy to take back. After several visits to the office in Oakland, including many complimentary dinners at a nearby Sizzler, we agreed to take the Armed Services Vocational Aptitude Battery (ASVAB), ten tests to determine if we were fit enough to serve our country. The portion that measured cognitive ability, much like an IQ test, proved we were learning something in college for the last several years.

We performed so flawlessly, we had our choice of every field to apply for. The physical test also proved our three-day-a-week social/gym hours at the university Rec Center built up enough of our endurance to pass us. None of us were disqualified for being pregnant. (Another girl in our small group got the unexpected news and boot out of the door, and I had to swear up and down to the doctor giving me my pelvic exam that he Absolutely Would Not be able to insert any tools inside of me because I was still, and determinedly so, a virgin. It took several minutes and talking to two nurses to convince the doctor I was not lying). I finished all the physical tests. I could even do a pull-up, but that wasn't required for the Army, just the Navy, and we had made the judicious, unanimous decision that this was the branch most supportive of our advancement as women.

ॐ

Interesting thing, that book *The Bell Curve*. The IQ tests the authors use in their research came from a study began in the 1980s of thousands of young Americans. It was called the National Longitudinal Study of Youth (NLSY) conducted by the U.S. Department of Labor's Bureau of Labor Statistics. The participants of this study took the ASVAB, the same test we took to try and join the Army. Some critics of these armed forces tests claim that they are a measure of ability to perform certain cognitive skills required in the military, not overall intelligence, so the results are not as relevant as the authors claim.

What I remember is that one of the cognitive tests seemed impossible to pass. We were told how many minutes we had to answer an overwhelming number of questions. When we began, I did a quick calculation of how much time I had per question to try and figure out each multiple choice answer. The answer was a mere few seconds. If I had to read each question, analyze the answers, and then choose the best one, I would never finish the questions.

I fell into a vortex. It was one of those movie moments from "A Beautiful Mind" where the ultra-genius but mentally tormented mathematician, John Nash, looks at a newspaper and can see the letters swirling off of the page in double-helixical patterns, showing him much "higher" information—even clues to government espionage and possibly the universe—than what is printed on the page. The longer I stared at the page, the more the questions and answers became a lucid grid, and a pattern revealed itself. I made a decision to trust that instinct, and without reading the questions or answers, I followed the back and forth pattern, pointing my finger here and there and here again, and finished that test with time to spare.

We received our scores soon after. I received the highest score possible on that part of ASVAB (I bombed the test on mechanics—I didn't even know if the pictures of engines and parts of cars or planes or Area 51 spaceships were right side up), but I can tell you this: I can't tell you one letter of what I was being tested on in the cognitive portion of it all.

ℰↄ

The final interview was with an old staunchy guy behind a government desk. He asked me about my personal health history and rattled off a list of diseases to see if I had any of them. A chorus of "no, no, no sir, no, no" sang from my mouth. He got to bronchitis; I said I had it once when I was in sixth grade, and he took a long pause, started pointing his pen at me.

"Are you sure it was bronchitis and not asthma?"

I remembered my sister, a nurse, telling me how to define these diseases, and that the suffix, "–itis" meant "inflammation of" and then whatever it was modifying.

I told him, in a rare move of verbal confidence while facing authority (i.e. old, white people), "Yes—I'm sure it was bronchitis, because bronchitis is the inflammation of one's bronchial tubes, and that's what the doctor diagnosed me with. It was NOT asthma. I have never had asthma, sir."

He was annoyed but respected my answer. He did one final sweep-check of my visual features—eyes, tongue, hands, posture, and then he looked at my ear and found the only dry spot on my body at that time. He asked me if I knew it was there, and I said I wasn't aware of it (I was clearly hiding my eczemic history for reasons I wasn't sure of—perhaps it was instinct that something about having this skin disease was as condemnatory as having asthma—a fact I did find out later to be true). He told me that until it was proven otherwise, that tough, dry spot on my left earlobe looked like eczema, and that I was denied the opportunity to enlist in military duty to our country. I was immediately offended and tried to argue, but I knew his eagle eye had found a kink in my armor.

As I walked out of the office and into the waiting room where our recruiting officers, now friends, were waiting, I told them my verdict. They weren't surprised and told me they are very aggressive at rejecting anyone with any history of asthma or skin diseases because they would be liable to provide health care for us for the rest of our lives even if we only served the first ten minutes in the military. Chronic diseases like that don't usually kill people, but they would need long-term healthcare that the military didn't want to fork out no matter how book-smart the person may be.

I had to wait a long while because Sonya chose to join ROTC, and Michelle immediately enlisted into the Army. She was in an adjoining room, perhaps with other hapless youth, taking the most serious oath of loyalty to honor, protect, and serve our country in times of peace as well as in times of war.

Eventually, I would try to appeal my denied enlistment by going to Kaiser to get records and/or a letter from my doctor to waive my eczema liability. I even drafted a letter as a legal document promising I would not use my eczema—if it ever flared up while in the military—to be discharged and then dependent on them for chronic disease healthcare. My doctor said she couldn't write the letter because all of my health records from as far back as my toddler years recorded eczema rashes on different parts of my body. After reading the desperate letter I had written, envious that Michelle was already scheduled for Basic Training in Texas and Sonya was marching and drilling across Cal's campus, accruing units to become an officer upon graduation, I panicked. Prayer occurred to me, so I submitted to it.

Writer Anne Lamott says our prayers are basically boiled down to, "Help me, help me, help me" or "Thank you, thank you, thank you." I waxed the former prayer.

I got a sense of pause, an ability to breathe in my frantic resolve to get to the place I thought I was headed for. I let a day pass, then another, and then a week was gone, and a month. The letter stayed in my backpack, and I never visited our recruiting officers again to let them know what they had already known and moved on from: I was not meant to join the Army.

A year later, President Clinton cut the military significantly, closing all the military bases in the Bay Area within the coming months. Thousands of soldiers were "fired" or "laid off." Michelle was off the hook, and off her path to a military-paid nursing degree. Sonya flew through the last two years of ROTC, and after many of her sorority sisters—including me, her roommate in the House—received phone interviews from secret government individuals who would not disclose anything to us but kept asking us the most intimate details about our ringleader, designated sacrificial hoe (DSH*), and funniest drunk to fall off a scooter

---

* DSH—Designated Sacrificial Hoe. We made that term up especially for Sonya. She was the girl who would approach a table full of guys, flirt with them, get free drinks, and then invite the rest of us, coyly leering at a distance, to join in the flirting. Sonya had an introductory line. She'd walk up to the cutest guy in the crowd and say, "Hi, I'm Ruby. My friend way over there will sit on your lap for a quarter." It was outrageous,

as part of a normal day in the life of, she disappeared to do intelligence in Korea. I saw her once years later while I was living in Hawai'i, and she was stationed there briefly before her next secret assignment. She was the same two-stepping, dyed-Alf-orange-haired hot Mexican anomaly in cowboy boots with the blondest, bluest-eyed officer boyfriend loving her. She was sent away again, and from Florida, she sent a postcard to Patricia from Disneyworld with two lines: "I'm in Florida after Korea. I have a new boyfriend who I am in love with (duh!). Things are crazy here. –Sonya."

That was the last we saw or heard of her.

୧୭

On this curve, scoring so high on the ASVAB's IQ tests, and being at the very top of the bell curve, didn't mean anything; I was totally unprepared for the military. If these were the tests the book based research on, I think about the fresh 18 year-old kids taking the tests. Were they just as unsure of themselves and their capabilities as I was at 21? Or worse? Did they study for the test or get a good night's sleep and eat a well-balanced meal that morning? Did they care to think that ten, fifteen years later, the test they took would end up informing a book that basically doomed certain races?

୧୭

When I finally finished at Cal (or it finished with me), I left with a B.A. in English. I entered undergrad as a sparkly-eyed Bio major with neither plan nor purpose for the degree except maybe to travel around the world helping people construct miniature ecosystems or three-dimensional cell models. When I stopped eating red meat and noticed I was subconsciously rescuing vagrant bottles, cans, and plastic empties from streets and garbage bins by the backpackful (to my friends' and sisters' reproach, especially after last call at the bar), I changed my major to

---

but we're sure the guys didn't care what she was saying. A hot, exotic Mexican girl was breathing on them. She got us drinks, limo rides, hotel rooms when we couldn't drive home, and free meals.

Conservation Resource Studies*. After major budget cuts to education (again, sigh), CRS was whittled down to a few classes here and borrowed (reused) equivalent environmental classes from there, and I switched to English Literature. I should have owned up to this, as my consistent bell-bottom grades of Cs and Ds (and occasional "I," or Incomplete, grades) in all the Science and Math classes were predicting what would be my educational fate. If I was unable to slide past the bell hump on any test or assignment, I would not have been able to excel in careers related to science or even recycling. Right?

I signed up and worked for the San Francisco Conservation Corps under the umbrella of Americorps—the urban version of the Peace Corps—teaching, supervising, and mentoring at-risk teens from 11–18 years old. I fifteen-passenger-vanned them around the San Francisco Bay Area to beautify and restore neighborhoods by landscaping public parks, painting out graffiti, stocking food banks, visiting senior citizens, and cleaning up beaches. I designed and taught English, Art, Creative Writing, and Math classes. Respecting our environment was an ethic we wove into all of our curricula. With my partial recycling degree and ongoing habit of picking up aluminum and #1 or #2 plastics from anywhere, the fever caught with my assigned Crew of Junior Corps Members (plus, I bribed them with a snack for every five recyclables they brought into work each morning). The year and a half I was a Crew Leader, Crew 17 won a pizza party each semester for blowing the other crews out of the water with our impressive recycling poundage.

While such a transformational joy to be part of, I could not relate to most of the students' personal and academic burdens. Even though many of the refugee children (from Cambodia and Laos) looked very much like my cousins, and our family consistently had recently-immigrated cousins living with us until they could get stable, I couldn't find common ground with these immigrants. These kids were frequent runaways or in homes with absentee single parents who worked minimum wage or illegal jobs all day to provide for their many children and often, grandchildren. Or, if they were Mexican-American, they were succumb-

*CRS—basically a hoity-toity college label for "recycling" major.

ing to peer pressure all over the Mission District's territorial, gang-affili-
ated streets. A few students in my care had secret abortions at 12 or 13;
another was known as the drug dealer of his block (I could never prove
it, even if he showed off fist-sized rolls of cash and new basketball shoes
every week).

Ideally, if the program functioned as it was designed, these kids used
their work permits and were paid minimum wage to learn life skills and
truthfully, to have their own spending and food money, so their parents
or older siblings could use their incomes to pay hospital and electricity
bills, renew bus passes. There were a few kids in our program who did
get straight As and whose stunting naïveté very much reminded me of
how I lived my teenage life. But the fact that their parents allowed them
to work for our program—as they lived in Section 8 housing alongside
everyone else, many of them collecting welfare checks—showed they
were far from as sheltered as I was.

I have lost touch with most of the teens in the program. But a sober-
ing thought remains that some of the paths these kids were on when I
left led them straight into harm's way. In this light, how could anyone
doubt that socioeconomic factors speak volumes more than an IQ test
thrown at them? What's the bottom line, then, for how to make sure
these kids grew Up and not Away?

I would bet that, if these kids were surrounded by any positive, core
community or even a single, steadfast mentor—like a parent who was
able to stay home long enough to talk with or do homework with them,
or like Bob was investing his life in young Berkeley boys—regardless of
what grades they earned in school or even how they would land on any
bell *or* belle curve, those who used this visceral, street-tested intelligence
and made it, really *made it.*

Now, as a tutor at San Diego City College, the classes look similar
to the international faces back in San Francisco. The difference is about
twenty or thirty, even forty years of age (or more) between those Americorps teens and the City College students. In City's classes are ex-con-
victs making honest efforts to learn how to read, write, and argue an idea
with more rhetorical strategies than fighting or stealing. There are single

parents (and pregnant teens) disciplined enough to work jobs, raise their children, and try to take full course loads. Seats at the English Center are filled with refugees from war-torn countries—some taking the same Chemistry and Biology classes I failed, but these students are successfully getting top grades while listening to lectures and reading textbooks in a language they just learned (or are learning simultaneously). I look at the young students who are uncomfortable in this environment because it doesn't look like high school anymore, and I wonder if they will ever grasp the Gift being in these surroundings is for them. They get to see their potential future, good or bad, eye to eye.

ℰ∽

This is where an awesome, well-drawn, all-encompassing conclusion would be. There would be slick answers to the questions raised by the issues around a bell/belle curve, meant to determine who was on top, who was at the bottom, and who would settle in as average. Where does intelligence—academic, social, relational, intuitive—really come from? How is it developed? Mutated? Honed? Dwarfed? Mismanaged? Snuffed out? How could it really be measured? Is there such a way?

And of those who are measured by a bell curve, what are all those people—those top-o-the-bell-mornin'-to-ya *geniusi* from my college years—doing today? Do they have careers and families? What would their peers say about their smartness? What about their spouses and children? What about their paychecks? Do they believe their children, too, will be successful because they are just the right shade of human?

And what about the scientific racism of that book? I'd like to use my Bizarro-world mountains of free time to collect and analyze data that shows it's all B.S. But then what about what's happening today in education? The experts are calling the inequities in educational resources for certain races and incomes the next civil rights issue. There was a professor on TV, a Black American graduate from an Ivy League college, who has launched pilot programs to close this Achievement Gap in ethnic populations. Apparently, only fifty percent of Black and Latino kids who enter high school finish with a degree. All the after-school and during-school programs to tutor and mentor these low-scoring groups haven't been working. So, this professor is trying a good old fashioned merit system of *Ch-ching*. A few high schools in Washington, D.C. and New York are paying their predominantly Black and Latino kids cash for every "A" they get in a class. Not just on report card day, but every five weeks, they get $50 for each progress report of an A.

Man, that's quite a bribe. Seriously. Now, when relating this to raising children, some experts say why reward the child for behavior that is expected? Why say, "If you clean your room and eat all your vegetables, you can have some ice cream" when children should be expected to keep their belongings in order and eat nutritious food without question? (And we don't have time to get into what rewarding good behavior with desserts might do for a young person's health and body-image down the road...) The books say that if we bribe our kids at this age, they will never learn to value achieving something for the sake of achievement alone. There'll always be a payday involved, an open hand waiting to get what we're training them they "deserve."

Here's where I'd use supporting data to say we're creating entitled kid monsters that grow into entitled teenage and young adult bloodsuckers whose only worth comes from being paid to do well. Blah blah percentage from this-n-that institution that we're creating a generation of hard working hoop-jumpers who produce nothing of real value; as long they get paid to perform, the end result is moot. We should stop perpetuating this system, right? Take the high road, let the kids cry when they don't get ice cream or $300 every five weeks for straight As. Make them realize, when they end up homeless and visionless, as they're panhandling on the streets or collecting welfare checks, that the learning in itself was the Golden Egg.

Then what do I do with the data I did find that shows Asian Americans as a whole are graduating almost all who enter high school, upwards of 90% compared to the 50% for Blacks and Latinos? Because if I was paid for my grades, and my cousins and their cousins were paid—in money, in shopping sprees, in material goods, in new cars for Sweet 16, in rare, public parental approval—you know this high success rate can be traced back to that open wallet and dangling carrot from mom and dad (along with, no doubt, the intrinsic immigrant fear of failure that drives this behavior from our parents). Something's right about this wrong way to raise our kids, too, because a lot of the students who set the bell curves in academics are Asian Americans. Even if the 90% rate plummets to 50% of Filipino Americans finishing a four year degree (unique to us Flips in the Asian category is that in our confused identity struggles—as this essay demonstrates—we do not uphold the "model minority" too well), for most of those who graduate, they do it with top honors. Many go on to medical, business, law schools. Then, they earn more degrees, more money and more accolades because the knowledge stuck and worked for them. And when they have their kids, you can bet this system will continue except with even more digitalized video game and sound systems to choose from.

So why not try to pay off our failing students to memorize more dates and diagrams? Why not extend it to pay for those of us trying to make it on the Belle curve, too? I'd put in a good extra hour to coif my hair and spackle my face with make-up. I'd get extra tutoring for social etiquette and secret maps of where to find the elite crowds to hobnob with. I'd marry "properly," raise my younguns, and keep my minivan tank full. I'd be a kept woman, but I'd know how to pass the horse-doovers.

Here, I keep writing until a brilliant resolution peeps through. And I draw some metaphor about the bell being made of gold, but then as people really investigate it, they notice it's just a patina. Or, it's just gold foil wrapper, and the bell is really chocolate, not at all as serious as people made it to be when they set out to determine test grades and write books meant to predict our fate.

The bell begins to toll, first at a distance where only the echoes are heard, the reverberations felt only by the hairs on our arms. Then, as the gongs get louder and more deafening, without exchanged words, we understand, well, for whom it tolls.

Brain to Mouth

Your brain ever "eat" something first, while it's still being transported to your mouth, but when your tongue encounters it, it's a counterfeit of what you predicted? Once, lunching, I sidestepped Desserts, preferring bowled fresh fruit. Only, as cubed melons kissed my lips, the façade materialized. I tasted some *kind* of fruit, but not the fruit I anticipated, deserved. Thwarted, I recommitted to trusting instinct: order crème brulee. These brain-to-mouth fake-outs are like dating. You re-promise yourself, no more "casting pearls to swine." Then, you date someone on the Red Flag hitlist. It's the bowl of imitation fruit all over.

Café du Monde

Papa was right when I told him I was going to visit New Orleans. I thought he was paranoid when he told me that I wouldn't feel comfortable in the South. Why did I ignore him when he said they don't serve him and his Filipino Navy "buddies" in restaurants in Alabama or Georgia on their stationed leaves? And this has been true for over twenty-five years since he's been in the military? The last time, they told him they don't serve "brown folk his kind" in a restaurant somewhere in Louisiana.

11 July 1993 — Café du Monde, New Orleans

I can't believe I'm only two hours away, here in this metropolis of ideas and cultures, from Hell. Shaun took me to meet his cousins on his mom's side so that I could meet some of his family before we get married next year. It wasn't a big deal to me that two of his second cousins married each other; first and second cousins marry each other all the time in the Philippines to keep the money in the family so I thought, what's the big deal?

When we got there, his cousin Annette was cooking food for us. She made no eye contact with me, but I didn't think it was because she couldn't stand my color. Shit. Can you believe it? I went to the bathroom, and while there I could hear them talking, interrogating Shaun.

I could hear Joseph, Annette's cousin-husband, talking in his Looserana drawl.

"So Shaun, what is she? I never seen anyone like that before." I heard nothing from Shaun. "I mean, she ain't one of us, that's for sure, but she ain't no nigger either."

I heard Annette say from the kitchen's direction, "Maybe she's more like one of those *sand* niggers. They come in all different looks."

I opened the door to step out, and they stopped talking. Shaun was speechless; I could tell by his face. I know he wanted to defend me, but he wasn't prepared for this. He finally said, as we sat down to home-cooked red beans and rice (that Annette bowled out from a big, industrial pot with a two-foot long hambone sticking out) "Ella's a Filipino."

I corrected Shaun, "Filipina-American. American." I don't know why I added that.

I tried my best to drown the entire event, to hover over the situation like I used to pretend to do when I heard mom and papa fighting, threatening to leave each other, and I had to sit there trying not to cry while swallowing broccoli beef and rice.

Joseph noticed I was spacing and said, "You never been to a real farm before, huh?"

At least he's talking to me, I thought desperately. "No, it's such a large piece of land. How do you get to the supermarket or the store when you need something?" I didn't want to hear an answer; I just wanted the meal to end so I could run out of there.

He sat up, suddenly acting interested. "One thing we like to do — I forgot to tell you this Shaun for when you come hunting for deer with us in Georgia — is that, when our shells get old — we don't like to keep rifle shells for more'n a year because then some of 'em don't work when we try to shoot 'em — we take the shells, and I mean boxes and boxes of 'em, the boys and me, to some of the nigger neighborhoods and drop 'em on the street out the windows of our trucks."

Shaun and I were visibly perplexed, but I was more stunned by his nonchalant use of the "N" word. I couldn't speak. Shaun asked for us, "Why do you do that?"

Joseph shoveled a large spoonful of beans into his mouth, answering while he chewed, "We figger if we can't out and out shoot 'em dead, maybe they'll find our shells and kill each other!"

He laughed with his mouth hanging open, punching Shaun in the shoulder while his beans and rice oozed molten from the corners of his mouth. Annette got up to fill his plate with more slop.

While this happened, Shaun was pursing his lips, and I was trying to scream for help from behind my eyes, my teeth, my skin. Then, in a glitch, Joseph stopped smiling and laughing, leaned forward as if he recognized something in me—maybe my horror I thought, so I grabbed Shaun's hand under the table—and he rested his chin on his elbow-propped hand. I could see the motor oil stains on his curled fingers. I felt I might vomit.

He kept staring quietly now, and as Annette returned to the table, he winked at me and said, "Ohhh, now I know who **you** are. I remember 'Nam."

I don't know the next thing that happened except we were driving back down from Thibodaux to New Orleans. I was in so much shock I couldn't react, certain that my spirit was savagely raw, mutilated around the edges, open.

And there they were. The holes, exposing the thing, that Thing I couldn't name but suspected was in me: dark, hot, better left uncultivated.

Arroz Caldo Recipie

This is a Filipino "rice stew," as we kids called it growing up. It literally translates "hot rice," and is found simmering on stove tops during family gatherings. Our family never ate it alone; it mostly fed the dozens of kids buzzing around the house and yard while our parents played blackjack or mahjong until two or three in the morning (who knows if they ate at all).

2 to 3 lb. cubed chicken—preferably dark meat, but use the breast if
    you like
3 tbsp. vegetable or corn oil—olive oil if you want to be healthier
2 tbsp. minced garlic
¼ cup chopped onion
½ inch ginger finely diced (you can simply slice it if you like, but kids
    hate biting into a chunk of ginger when their brains are thinking,
    "Mmm, chicken")

NOTE: you can use standard measurements, or you can use my relatives and stepdad's measuring tool: use your thumb to point to different digits on your forefinger. For example, a ½ inch of ginger is the distance from the finger tip to the first joint your thumb reaches. Two tablespoons of garlic is equivalent to the thumb pointing to the middle knuckle.

6 cups water
2 cups uncooked short-grain rice
¼ cup chopped scallion
salt or patis (fish sauce) to taste (you can get patis in most metropoli-
    tan supermarkets)
¼ tsp. freshly ground pepper

Heat oil, brown garlic, and sauté onion and ginger. Add chicken and salt or patis. Simmer approximately five minutes. Add water and rice. Simmer over low heat for 20 minutes or until rice and chicken are tender. Stir often to prevent sticking.

Scoop into bowls. Garnish with fresh pepper and chopped scallion. (Let the kids decide if they want the scallions; they have enough to contend with avoiding the ginger!)

♥

Interesting Thoughts I Have When Making This Dish:

#1 – The first Filipinos to come to the United States came to Loui-
siana swamps, escaping the Manilla Galleon Trade, as early as the late 1700s. They stayed discreet, but they have left their mark on Louisiana's history. Some of them even fought for the famed Jean Baptiste Lafitte under Andrew Jackson in the Battle of New Orleans, War of 1812.

#2 – A circulated point of pride is that Filipinos gave the word, "boondock" to Louisianans and the South. The Filipino (Taga-
log) word for "mountain" is "bondoc" (pronounced *buhn-DOK,* short 'o' sound in second syllable).

#3 – Rice is an import from Asia. How different in purpose (comfort food) and at family gatherings (easy to stretch sparse ingredients to feed many) is *Arroz Caldo* from *Red Beans and Rice*?

Reprints

What can I say to you? In leaving you've left. Did I make things too easy for you? My willingness to actively love you stop you dead in your tracks, turn you 180? Did you make your move during the night while I dozed? I called your name, just a dust above a whisper, because I saw you behind my eyelids. How, when you're talking across a room, I watch your lips and get thirsty for a long, engulfing drink of your kisses. A flash of light hits your eyes, angles down your neck, lights the ends of your hair into tiny golden flames, and I wonder whether it's from the sun outside or the luminescence from your very marrow in that heightened pause in the now. Is any of that brilliance able to be soaked in by me? Have you ever felt the full weight of your loneliness during those rare but echoing self-quakes in life? When the world magnifies all around you as you remain the minority of one, do you look down at your feet and see the platform you're standing on is a blood-drawn, sweat-drenched handmade pedestal with me below, adoring?

Every now and then I see too clearly through the muck: how I can't love you anymore because I can't love you any *more*.

Do you yet know? Exactly how long did I impress you? Enough to skirt from interest to undress to unrest? Strange tears, they come and go, like your tidal presence. While being neither here nor there, lost. While being neither here nor there, found. So much of me was learning to feel honest, arcing towards behind whole. Then the eruption, and it drained away into the other, *that* hole. Winked at me there in the Something Nothing.

I am dumbfounded; I pray for forgiveness of self. My mind wondering amidst your hands' wanderings. Frozen in flashback, unable to forget. I stare at the pictures: reprints of wishful thinking and concrete insecurities.

&

Y'didn't think I'd remember, did you? But ooh honey, I remember just like I walked out your bedroom—hair tied up, backpack monkeying a ride on one shoulder, tore up 501s, used and reused, just like I was feeling. Don't you know I took home pictures of you and me from those nights?

Foolish me, I wanted you to scratch my back like Mom did every night to help me sleep help me feel cared for help me. And like always, the electricity of your fingers charges me, pulses throughout, and I'm shocked when the effect wears off and you, you climb off me leaving me, me to climb out of my disbelief. The picture of your satisfied sleepiness wins me over, and I'm convinced for the next few hours you want to be with me; you choose to love only me.

The ride home is blurry, like the pictures. I got some shots of that loneliness, too. Head half-cocked, I pull my hair down to feel hidden, [invisible], safe. Walk to the door, too lazy to unload the things I hid in my backpack before I walked through your door: Dignity; Self-knowledge; Shame. Inside I drop to the couch, curl up my knees, turn on the TV so it can watch me, watch me without judging. The buzzing finds the shallow, empty fissures and fills them for now.

I shove a world's worth of clamoring chaos down inside the grooves.

Later y'see, I'm gonna try and print these pictures. Put them in my album and file it back on top the dusty shelf where it belongs, where I want it to belong. I wanna think it was all good, that *we oughtta be in pictures*, that we'd wanna enlarge some of the shots even, or just make copies. Live it all over one more time, make it Okay.

But sweetheart, we both know what's up. And no matter what we say or do, the truth is the only things we got to make these reprints from—well, they're all negatives.

Surf Baptism

I'm paddling hard, even
as my undisciplined arms
drown in fatigue and numbness.
They're cold, bloated—some karma,
another lifetime's torture,
I swear I do *not* deserve.
He told me I would hate it,
that I'd use every last nerve
to get out to the lineup.
I'd curse at the sea, swearing
to God, **this is the last time.**
He warned as he waxed, daring
me through a lopsided smile.
I took the board, leashed myself,
hand over hand digging deep
out towards the ocean's shelf.
It's been long since that season
when we shared more than the sun
and a few waves. I still feel
that watery resurrection,
somehow smoothing dark, rough edges
into glass. In my truck, sand
sucks my thighs, grinds through my hair,
settles around bare feet and
floor mats. My stomach growls. I
drive home, glad to be hungry.

weather forecast

high 70s to low 80s and clear inland
low 70s beaches—marine layer in a.m. giving way to afternoon sunshine

on the answering machine my sister scattered
a pile of glass for me to gulp down
call me as soon as possible
i chewed
i bled
i dialed and spat

it's "invasive lobular carcinoma" i'm not sure what that all means her
left breast mom's overwhelmed that's why i'm calling behind the nipple
the size of a silver dollar i suggested she have them both removed just
in case just in case mammograms only find half of them we won't know
about chemo and radiation until after they check her nodes can you
come up next week we'll have your birthday here and you can play with
the girls they miss you we didn't expect a visit until april the baby's here
say hi to your auntie she's grumpy i better go put her down for her nap
i'll call you tomorrow

                                                                    pray.

oh and it's the usual unpredictable weather do you have a warm coat
we never know these days see you soon

outside the sun all toasty
with its nose turned sideways
like bliss it smacks me ignorant
snides me saying who cares if it's winter
this is my kind of town
let them wear tank tops and carry sweaters

in their back pockets
those skeptics
still
the daylight's the only thing keeping me
from punching my head
through the coffee table's glare

i climb the stool in the closet
find the wool sweater out of reach
on the top shelf
sun fumes outside my window
tapping like fingers annoyed
unable to reach me
and burn at my pallid face
while the dross of my denial drips
my mouth sputtering red.

Professional Experience

Dear Scratchpad

May 2001

Dear Scratchpad*: I have had eczema all my life. In my case, it is an inherited, but manageable skin disease; when it came, it was localized in small, occasionally bothersome patches on my arms and legs. I have visited dermatologists for minor flare-up control, and that was the extent of my specific atopic dermatitis. Seven years ago, after a traumatic fall off of a 150 foot waterfall in Yosemite National Park, my reasonably dormant eczema began to eat me alive during my post-traumatic stress.

Throughout my doctors' visits, all dermatologists have nonchalantly quipped (quite hopelessly, I admit), "Most people have rashes that itch; you have itches that rash." They have sent me away with whatever steroidal ointment and oral med prescriptions I already had tubes and bottles of at home, telling me, "come back and see me in six months."

What has frustrated me the most through the years is how these medicines seem to only treat the symptoms, and even then the treatment is so fleeting. If I stopped taking a certain antihistamine that I had been taking every day for months, within a few hours, I'd be cursing my paper-thin, irritable skin. My M.O. is always: I itch and scratch, that skin becomes inflamed, loses pigment and elasticity, bleeds and cracks, and gets itchier. It spreads from arm to arm, chest to back, neck to face. I don't know what's worse, itching or hurting, and when I'm under attack I don't know the difference.

---

*The *Scratchpad* is a national newsletter disseminated by the National Eczema Association for Science and Education (NEASE). The newsletter's main goal is to share testimonials of sufferers of eczema.

On top of this legacy, I have also inherited allergies to cats, dogs, grasses, trees, and so many everyday foods it would be easier to list what I *can* eat rather than what I can't. Put all of these stressors into a five-foot three, flat-chested brown girl with frizzy hair, and it all crescendos until I'm ultimately unable to sleep, forbidden exposure to sun, water, or clothes that aren't loose-fitting and cool, and denied a working, functioning life. Wait, there's more. Since it is documented that emotional stress exacerbates physical symptoms, you can imagine the "shame spiral" I had been quickly co-opting.

The first attack of this magnitude (after Yosemite), I was given a reprieve invitation by my sister's family who lived on Oahu, Hawai'i. There, the dermatologist instructed me to dip into the ocean a few days a week to get the healing effects of salt water. She also told me that the continuous trade winds would help alleviate my allergies. For almost a year, it worked. I learned how to surf, and I watched the sun rise and set each day in the humid, freshly circulating air.

Soon enough however, I hit a plateau in my healing curve. After more allergy testing, I found out I'm allergic to every plant and tree blooming in Hawai'i, and I was reassured this would never improve because in tropical areas, plants and trees bloom year round. I have since moved to San Diego, California, the closest thing to Hawai'i, sans the island magic and bath-warm water. My own magic happened when I got married a few months ago to my quintessential surf partner and fellow writer. Here, I'm currently trying, once again, to heal from a second, more arduous attack than the one that propagated my move to the islands.

Undeniably, the most frustrating part of having this specific sickness is that it is different from individual to individual, between fifteen million of us in America, who have it. "Atopic" is Greek for "atypical or strange." I'm told by one of my several cousins who is in healthcare that there are more than 20 genes involved in this state of Atopy, and although we don't know how to cure it, at least we know that no two patients will have the same symptoms. It can attack different organs—someone's lungs, resulting in asthma, or another's nasal passages, hence hay fever for example. Or it can move around in the same person, say from the lungs to the skin, or to the lungs AND skin. Finding the source is as nebulous as finding the, a, any, or all cures. Doctors' "advice" resonates through my memory:

> *You have to live with this chronic illness for the rest of your life.*
>
> *There's nothing medicine can do about it right now.*
>
> *You can help manage it by finding what works for you to keep it down.*
>
> *Stop scratching or it'll stay;*
>
> *Stop scratching or you'll get secondary bacterial infections;*
>
> *Stop scratching or you'll trigger other skin conditions.*

In my arguably fatalistic, apocalyptic upbringing (Mom: "The Lord giveth, and the Lord taketh away," cousins: "It must be God's will to test you through this time," Dad: "God has a reason for everything"), this sickness—now going on ten straight months of "flare up"—has convinced me to take inventory of the role my disease has invariably assumed in my life. Notably, it has borrowed enough sick-leave from my "normal" life to cause me thought. Why so long, why now even after the wedding stress is over, why here in San Diego where I had all the environmental elements that healed me considerably in Hawai'i and then some?

కా

Earlier in the year, about three months into this current flare up, while trying to secure a photographer, a disc jockey, a florist, a makeup artist, and wedding party hotel accommodations for our wedding that was in less than two months, I crashed head-on into my wits' end. One of my bridesmaids answered a group e-mail plea for solace. She suggested, or rather begged, me to try Oriental medicine. She knew of an acupuncture clinic that is regarded as the best in the West Coast, and it was by no coincidence in Mission Valley, right here in San Diego.

Instead of opening myself up to the possibility of it helping, even curing me, I sat on it by spending time "researching" rather than acting on the advice.

Thousands of years old, acupuncture came from physicians in China and has now been warmly welcomed in the United States in the last three decades as a viable option to and/or integrative treatment with Western medical treatments. The main difference is that Western medicine boasts excellent treatment of trauma and symptoms of illness whereas Oriental medicine functions from the belief that every part of the human body—from the skin to the liver to points on the earlobe—plays an essentially life-giving role in making a person "balanced" and thus, healthy.

(Buzzword: holistic.)

Acupuncture uses hair-thin needles that are inserted into several points on the body believed to be responsible for such things as integrating organ function, triggering endorphins to pained areas, even blocking pain messages from reaching nerves that tell the brain about it.

Qi (pronounced "chee") is believed to help regulate balance in the body. It is influenced by the opposing forces of yin and yang, which represent positive and negative energy and forces in the universe and human body. Acupuncture is believed to keep the balance between yin and yang, thus allowing for the normal flow of qi throughout the body and restoring health to the mind and body (Acupuncture.com).

After a certified nervous breakdown due to continuous mounting pain, itching, and hopelessness, I gave in. In addition to all the online and brochure "research" I had done, I acquiesced, *what's the harm in trying this form of treatment?* Western therapies have repeatedly treated my symptoms over the span of my life, but apparently they weren't getting to the source of my sickness. Since this clinic used interns to treat patients while being supervised by a licensed, private acupuncturist, costs were only half of the private rate and thereby affordable for our soon-to-be-married diminishing income. A few months before the wedding, thousands of dollars spent on yet-visible vendors, and here I was red and puffy, a patchy insomniac whose dreams of the fairy tale wedding needed first a medical miracle riding in on a steed before her Prince Charming could make his entrance.

The doctor who saw me at the Oriental Medicine clinic immediately put her hand on my shoulder after looking confidently at my crusted over, inflamed, hypo-pigmented skin as if to challenge it to a draw. What she said directly to the skin, then to my doe-in-headlights eyes, and eventually to the intern who would be performing the acupuncture in bold voice was, "We will get this. Be patient, and we will get this."

We will get this. Be patient, and we will get this.

I have been going consistently, three days a week on the doctor's recommendations, drinking supplemental herbal teas that help to release "wind" from my imbalanced body. In Oriental medicine, "wind" is caused by heat in the blood, manifesting itself as bodily heat and inflamed body organs, of which the skin is the largest. (And incidentally, in defense of Western medicine, in the last three decades, it has been established that the skin is not just a barrier that keeps the "bad things" from coming "in" and the "good things inside" from leaking out. It is, in fact, the largest immunologic organ, vital in protecting us from harmful sun damage, bacteria, fungi, viruses and other invasives that the human body does not recognize as healthy.)

On a macroscopic level, acupuncture tries to balance what we've all heard and seen in trend as "yin" and "yang." It is believed that Western medicine treats the Yin while Oriental medicine, including acupuncture, treats the Yang in patients. To those who subscribe to Oriental philosophy, Yin and Yang have universal applications. Literally translated, the Chinese characters for Yin and Yang mean respectively, the "shady side of the hill" and the "sunny side of the hill." If this is true, I think it somewhat "meta"-ironic that I moved to San Diego to get more Yang, more of the "sunny side" of my existence, away from the concrete landscapes, the "shady" side, of the Bay Area and its heavy-handed introspection.

In elementary terms, although I have a measurably long way to go going this comprehensive route, I look forward to feeling better one day. Much, much better.

Closing Escrow

or

The Difference Between Owning and Renting

You can paint *every* wall a different color—*any* color you want—there's no security deposit! Go ahead and pierce the ceiling raw with hooks. Hang tea-lit paper lanterns and that miniature bamboo house, with shells for chimes, from mom's last trip to the Philippines; *your* place doesn't have the century-old way of electrical wiring coursing like veins up there. Store your surfboards in your *own* two-car garage, not behind your couch. And speaking of, no more parking tickets. Forget Street Sweeping Wednesdays!

Now, no one lives above or below you (although you do share one or two walls because you couldn't *quite* afford a "stand-alone" house with your pooled *DINK (double income, no kids)* status—are you kidding, here in the Impossible Housing Crunch capital of the nation—but you got the beach*nearish* condo after an unusually low-casualty bidding war, so you'll nurse those wounds on your Own two- by three-foot patio later, and you'll remember to give your next door neighbors the skinny on how you might have people over and blah yada blah). This means *get* the bigger, badder speakers. Two-step shamelessly to multi-Grammy winner Garth Brooks when you feel "a little bit country." Croon at the moon with your chords, strum and pluck your steel string, practice harmonies to Godsong melodies. Your women's support group, Babes in Christ ("A local, San Diego group that meets Tuesday nights in Ocean Beach for (vegan!) dinner, community, worship and prayer!") gets to *Praise you Jesus, Yes Lord, yes,* no holds barred, all night long. And when your husband surround-sounds all of his epics, inciting them to life, inviting tigers to ravage gladiators next to your new coffee table, or summoning hobbits and elves to defend the race of Man against all embodiments of Evil (just don't spill any Orc blood on the new sectional sofa) you can prep and steam your artichokes without having to tell him, *turn it down a few, y'know, downstairs neighbors.*

On the other hand...

You have to quarrel quietly now. Gone are the alleys where "You're driving me CRAZY" and "I can't STAND this shit," where "You're ALWAYS..." or "You NEVER..." are soaked up by stray cats or tossed into community dumpsters. You can't even blame it on the infamous wild parrots, asking people next morning if anyone heard *those damn birds* mimicking other people from *who knows what far off area of O.B.*, undomesticated, smug and bestial out there on top of telephone poles. Here, the neighbors will know you. (Should you muffle your lovemaking, too?)

Then, despite your "brave new world," "land of the free" decorating attitude, you become more careful about jamming nails blindly into walls, looking for studs. Calculator subtraction keys start punching in your head with each new nick. You become a mini-Scrooge, start imagining swooning equity. You change your mind about putting up the daring, ten by twelve-foot installation of a dozen smaller, mixed-media panels, designed and sketched in your journal when you first saw blank walls.

You contemplate reinstating the Asian *shoes-off-at-the-door* policy, but the Fu Man Chu Chinatown slippers mom used to have waiting by the front door may be strange to your eager *I'm-at-a-conference-in-Downtown-San-Diego-this-weekend-for-work...bringing-my-girlfriend... can-we-crash-at-your-place?* guests. You scribble a mental post-it to look through Sunday paper ads, see if there's a sale at Old Navy where you can buy plain, unassuming house slippers to offer. You don't want people to think you're foreign here.

You're owners now. You ate leftovers on Dinner Date Mondays, postponed trips to visit family in the Bay Area, scavenged quarters and dimes from winter coat pockets and dusty, special-occasion purses, cashed in Roth-IRAs and life insurance policies. You've slipped the Homeowners check in the mail on the way to Home *Despot* for more floodlights (the backyard click-rustle-shuffles when you're e-mailing after dark) and a welcome mat—maybe with a palm tree motif. Anyway, after today, you'll never have to lease someone else's home.

The Suitcase

I flew across four states the next week.
When I got there, I finally saw for myself
what they had pretended not to see
for the last fifteen years. There it was, taking
up the entire living room: one mammoth,
demoralized gray beast—a leathery
suitcase with ears, trunk, legs and eyes. It slumped
on the battered Persian rug, shyly weeping.
It was unaccustomed to being looked in the eye,
to being recognized, at last, for what it was.
Its eyes looked void, worn out by neglect,
a contradiction to its stuffed body, swollen
with all their baggage, waiting
to be unpacked.

Maggie overfed it with the last of her belongings,
stretch marks canvassing its old, distended body.
Its seams were punctured by the corners
of her favorite books, her gold-framed
picture of California, the last journal
she wrote in. She shoved it through the hallway
and into the living room.

When she awoke to the blurs
of pre-dawn, last night's tears
and too much wine, she tumbled over it.
The large, dreary mound heaved
next to the couch. Instead of screaming,
she let out a sigh. She supposed now,
she was too tired to make another excuse.

Besides, the poor creature had suffered long enough,
ignored by both of them, cramped in that tiny,
uninhabitable space. She needed a friend to get her
away from there. It was time for her to begin
the life she never started.

Homemade Cafe

It touches me there, the time-textured, paper-thin spot
in the upper left corner of my heart.
To see an "elderly" person sitting
two tables down   alone.
I wonder if that newspaper article is interesting
or is *no news good news*, but
any news is company?
Just like the plate of home fries with scrambled eggs
warmed up by a refillable cup of house coffee.
Breakfast in the middle of the day.
Is he hungry? For potatoes, or intimacy?
Maybe, like the Tuesday regulars, he has nobody to go home to,
but he did just six months earlier.

I thank God I'm not his waitress this time. Not today,
don't think I'm present enough to hear him grieve like the others.
All those times, bussing empty coffee mugs beside small,
heavy piles of napkin soaked with bereavement.

He gets up, I think to leave, and returns
with dessert and more coffee.

And now the mixed fruit torte mingles
glazed strawberries and kiwis
with spoonfuls of lost conversations
where sweet words were once
exchanged and devoured.

Kaua'i

She had been sleeping less and less since we got here. Seven days in Kaua'i, a gift from my new mother-in-law. She invited us to go with her and her husband to her timeshare in Poipu. Mom thought it would give us a second chance at our honeymoon.

Ella was too sick during our *real* honeymoon in Tahiti two months ago. She sat straw-hatted, wearing a printed, floral wrap, covering her skin from the sun and water while sitting in a beach chair under a palm tree. She watched as I snorkeled, and she waited with a book for me while I took boat rides around the smaller islands, the *motus*. As soon as we got there, I began begging her to try snorkeling, certain that if she put her head in the water in time to glimpse just *one* of the gorgeously-rainbowed fish—maybe even a stingray or a moray eel—she'd forget her pain. And when that worked, she could eventually go out wakeboarding every morning instead of watching the speedboats pull waterskiers and wakeboarders across our bungalow shoreview window.

She was getting antsy in no time, failing to stick with her belief that she shouldn't or couldn't because it might exacerbate her skin. By the third day, she was completely overrun by envy. She told me to get her snorkeling gear, and she put on her mask and fins. She walked out several yards on the shallow sea shelf and tried to snorkel with me, but being submerged for only one look into the reef, the salt water attacked the open wounds plaguing her entire upper body, and she was wailing in tears while I carried her, running, to the shower. I tried to tell her it was okay, that it wasn't a big deal, that we could do other things on the island. She softly rubbed medication into her back, chest, arms, neck, and face, and cried herself to sleep.

I couldn't touch her anywhere on her skin that week, our honeymoon, my wife.

ͼ϶

Last night, I was startled awake to see Mom rocking Ella back and forth—what must have been a vision from her childhood. As if she had a nightmare and needed grounding in reality, her mom's arms were trying to anchor her. She woke up in terror because her body had oozed iodine-colored liquid all over her pajamas, soaking through the pillow, flooding the sheets. This reaction had never happened before, so when she sat up to see why she was *sweating* in the air-conditioned room, her sudden scream summoned Mom from across the condo. I woke up to her distress, feeling doomed to incompetence.

I went swimming at the local beach while waiting for Ella to wake up from the night's ordeal, and I walked down the shore to watch eager tourists learning how to longboard. After a few hours, I returned to the condo to see if she was, fingers crossed, dressed and willing to leave the complex for the day.

She sat on the patio, a notebook in her hand, trying to write it seemed. I asked her in the most lighthearted voice I could conjure if she wanted to try and see Waimea Canyon, even have a picnic at the Na Pali Coast. It was just after lunch, still early enough to do both activities.

She didn't look up from her notebook. "I don't know. I don't care." She whispered. "I'm too tired to do anything, but if you want to, I'll sit in the car."

This was good to hear. I kissed her gently on the cheek. "You'll love seeing the island, sweetheart. The last time I was here, I promised myself I would go back to the Na Pali Coast because there wasn't enough time to explore even half of it!"

I packed our day bag with trail mix, water, and fresh-cut pineapple in tupperware Mom had left out on the counter with a note on it, telling us to take it, that she and her husband, Ella's stepdad, were out for the day being tourists. I took one of the coupon books that would save us some money if we wanted to stop at a restaurant to pick up to-go sandwiches or teriyaki bowls for the Coast. Ella packed her beach bag with meds—several travel-sized, recycled aspirin bottles full of pills and ointments that she refilled from industrial containers, as needed.

In the rental car, I turned on the AC for a couple of minutes to acclimate the interior for Ella. We decided to drive through the island first and see Waimea Canyon, then head over to the Na Pali Coast on the west side to catch the sunset. I pulled out the tourist guide map of Kaua'i and pointed out our route, smiling and reminiscing about the Garden Isle's grandeur.

"I can't believe we're here, for free, thanks to your mom—my new mom—where they filmed *Jurassic Park*!"

She nodded.

"I mean, you know me, hiking is what I could do *everyday*, *all* day, in the mountains, on the beach, up a cliff, *anywhere*!"

More nodding, a slight shoulder shrug.

We had been driving for less than half an hour, still having a while to go before we turned to go inland towards the Canyon, when I saw Ella turn her head out of the window, obviously impressed by the tropical paradise in front of her.

I handed her the point-and-shoot panoramic. "Take some shots!" I encouraged, "Yeah, if we can't go for long hikes up there, we can be the *other* kind of tourist and make a photo log for our scrapbook!"

I gestured towards the oceanscape with one hand and drove with the other. She timidly snapped two, maybe three pictures and put the camera, and her head, down.

I was going to recount the time I was in the Brazilian rainforest with my Best Man Mike, and how the mosquitoes were big enough to lasso and saddle up, but before I began my storytelling, I saw Ella's shoulders seizing, her head in her hands. She was weeping inaudibly.

I went silent.

Soon, her quiet tears rumbled, took form, and she was sitting up, rigid.

She rolled down her window and punched her fists through the hot, invading air, screaming at the top of her lungs.

"I FUCKING HATE THIS! I CAN'T FUCKING LIVE LIKE THIS!" She threw the map out of the window. I started to pull over.

"NO! Don't fucking stop! Just keep driving, get THERE. Get *SOMEWHERE*. I don't FUCKING care. I can't FEEL anything anymore! I can't SEE anything! I don't *WANT* to see anything!" She was starting to choke on her erratic breathing. I held one hand out to try and push her shoulders back into the seat, a *calm down* gesture, but she pushed me away and grabbed the roots of her hair, jerking.

"I want to DIE. I can't live like THIS. I mean, the doctors keep saying I have to accept *THIS*, that I'll have it *forever*, but that I can *control* it. CONTROL THIS? *How?!*"

She was beating on her skin, all over her body, howling recklessly. At the edge of hyperventilating, at the edge.

"I know EV-ER-Y FUCKING answer to this. I'm supposed to *LET* this ANGER pass. It's *NATURAL*, it's part of the *mourning process*. I'm supposed to FUCKING *MOURN* the death of my old, healthy self so that I can move on and ACCEPT my new life? ACCEPT THIS SHIT?! *HOW?*"

I didn't want to let go. I didn't want her to see me cry. She needed a stronger person to hold her up. *I* was her husband. *I* was that person. *I am that person.*

She kept screaming and crying, flinging her hands to the sky, yelling out of the window at the mountains, at the clouds, at God.

"*I DON'T WANT TO DIE TO MY OLD SELF*, God! I'm not ready to let go of the Old Me. I'm not ready to stop surfing, to stop hiking, to stop swimming and having a life! I don't have it in me! I've NEVER had to let go of those things! *What am I supposed to do?! I FUCKING hate my life!*"

I tried to comfort her, barely able to push out the words through my weak voice. "Ella, it's only for *now* the doctors say. They say it can get better, and it *probably* will. They only want you to accept these limitations for *today* so you can have a better attitude." I was talking to the sky, too, but this time it seemed devoid of the mountains, the clouds, God.

Ella continued to scream, over and over, "*This ISN'T me! This ISN'T me!*" She cried all the way to Waimea Canyon, and when we got there, she never got out of the car. I stepped out at vistas, taking quick shots of the view, convinced that she wouldn't look at these pictures with any morsel of fondness when they were developed.

I thought about being restricted from indulging in my passion for interacting with the outdoors. First Tahiti, now this also-perfect island. I walked to the border of the canyon, remembering my last trip there. An old friend and I took a hopper plane from Mau'i for a spontaneous over-nighter. We saw the canyon first, at about the same time judging from the sun's castings. I didn't want to sleep. The canyon walls mirrored the Grand Canyon, but this reflection exuded a richer, deeper, more verdant panorama. I imagined stepping out over the edge, filling the canyon with something meaningful. I wanted to stay so badly, I could taste the soil at the back of my throat. It was so cavernous, the feeling, all of it.

I gritted my teeth and tried to stave off anger at the thought that *I didn't agree to this*, this was not what I wanted to have to deal with. Were the rest of our lives going to be this constant emotional negotiation of, "sorry, she can't do it, so we both can't do it"? I loved her, but was I resilient enough to love us both through this?

She had screamed herself hoarse and was coughing and blowing her nose while we turned on the freeway towards the Na Pali Coast. She started breathing at an even pace; maybe peace was with her in some form. She leaned her head down on the car door window, now rolled up, and closed her swollen eyes. I watched her in my periphery as I continued driving west. Soon, her worn out body surrendered her into much-needed sleep.

I drove in a haze.

I didn't know what to do. I had always been the survivor in my family. If I persisted long enough, I would make it out okay, even happy. When my dad stole our savings and left my mom and me for another woman, and we had to move to Lake Tahoe with my uncle, while mom was signing us up for welfare, I borrowed a car and a friend drove me down to the comic book store with my comic books. I sold my thousand-book

collection and gave mom a handful of bills for us, no time to think or
rationalize. That was the first time; I was thirteen. Since then, I have
constantly been the one to bail people out, to save, to ease emotions.
Now, I can barely put two thoughts together since she got sick. I am
completely lost, not just unsure of whether I can help this time, but not
even knowing *what* that help is, or *where* to find anyone who had the
answer.

In the pit of my stomach, I began to feel a solid, rising mass emerge.
It rose steadily and lodged itself in my chest, filling my rib cage completely. After a few deep breaths, the feeling began to loosen up, each
cell expanding centrifugally, spreading outward. Warmth took over, and
I opened my mouth, lifting up my chin to extend my neck as it passed
through into my cheeks, eyes, and ears. My body began to tingle in
an increasingly pronounced way, a sort of burgeoning carbonation, and
the individual cells turned, washed over by this wave, no longer con-
strained.

The saltiness reached my mouth, dripped off of my nose before I
could acknowledge what was happening. I picked up the bottom edge of
my t-shirt and wiped at my eyes, trying to drive smoothly. I didn't want
to wake her. I drove towards the coast waiting for the tears to stop, but
they didn't.

There, I pulled over onto the dirt road to begin the unpaved drive
to the shore. The bumps jostled Ella awake, and she turned faintly to
see where we were. She looked at me long—both of us, eyes shiny and
bloodshot. She looked for the map, and when she didn't find it, she
reached for my hand carefully, her gaze fixed through the windshield.

The Psychofiles

Some patient files are so thick. But the thickest ones,
so much girth you could cut them open and count their rings,
are behind the wall of files you see through the receptionist's window.
The trick switch, I figured while waiting for my co-pay receipt,
is under the three-inch tall ceramic basset hound with, well yes,
puppy dog eyes, a Sherlock Holmes hat, a fetched (or smoked?) pipe,
and a wagging tail if you stare long enough,
on top of the computer monitor.

If you wait until the last head case sniffles stiffly out
and press the dog's tail, the entire file wall backbends.
There's a crawl space underneath.
Follow the Crayola-ed "burnt sienna" light a foot or so to the right,
there's the staircase. The descent isn't long or especially scary,
or as the docs might diagnose, *traumatic*.
It's more interesting than anything,
not so much a dungeon as a moldy, outdated,
tryst-central Motel 6 room.

There are sooooooo many files—
an entire high school hallway's worth of juicy, six-dollar-burger-thick files,
some so chock-a-block they look like accordions at full stretch.
Wanna know what *did* creep me out a twitch or two,
made my legs do an auto-180 and make for cover?
These files, they belong to the docs.

I didn't make it to the end of the hall, but I hear from an old-timer
(a 28-year old woman bipolar since 13—thanks in part, they say,
to a heroin mother and the mercury plant next to the projects)
that there are jars and jars of "stuff"—

lusting eyeballs, wandering hands,
irreverent tongues, overzealous peckers.

Back then, I imagine that was all in a day's work.

The Writing Well

Welcome to our collection of works, most our own, others we shared
in through personal visits and readings, and a sprinkling of other
writing for posterity's sake.

Whodaknown this class couldwouldshouldDID produce such a
memorable body of work? We journalled, we struggled with forms,
we wrote and rewrote, we threw it to the curb in rebellion, we
dragged ourselves to readings, then we got up there at open mics and
read our own pieces(!), and we even did our own reading in final
form at the end of this ride.

I'll say it now, you all should've spoken up even MORE in class.
There was so much to share.
is so much more to share.
will be.

With this in mind, we gladly look back, like proud-to-bake-our-first-
cake kids, on our Fall 2001 Semester of drawing deep,
sitting on the edges,
looking in at our reflections,
even when
we didn't want to at 9 in the morning.

If each day falls
inside each night,
there exists a well
where clarity is imprisoned.
We need to sit on the rim
of the well of darkness
and fish for fallen light
with patience
—*Pablo Neruda*

This. The introduction page for our class reader, the Intro to Creative
Writing class I taught last Fall. What did we call it? *"(out of the, fishing
from a, the, a, into the, on) Writing Well,"* that was it. Fumes and fear
got this publication to the campus printer. I can't even say I pulled off
the cool veneer by importing tiny icons of a notepad and a pen, choosing
electric blue for the bound cover page, sticking these trying-to-be-trendy

lines, *align right*, whatever's not Times New Roman font, on first turn. The students had to see me get that eczemic shade of "red puffier'" by the day three times a week, lose pigment in my forehead, mouth, cheeks, neck, followed by suicidal eyebrows plucking themselves out before my manic fingers hooked them out of form. I prayed to God this passive book on their shelves replaced all those memories as soon as they got their grades. *If they recall me at all, God, let it be as a feeling of compassion for their writing lives, for their lives, without a body to encase it.* Maybe the only thing that was true (or true-ish) in the book was the bigger font, *larger than life*, effect.

Larger than life—so consuming I don't remember details of the publication, if I even read it post-production. I still have their original work in stacks entombed in our apartment closet. I had to beg for forgiveness through boomeranged e-mails when they asked me why their portfolios weren't graded and returned with comments, with any kind of paw print or spaghetti-stain proof that I touched them before I made final grades.

Early December made over half a year of three-hour sleepfits. We'd given up on acupuncture after I almost barfed up the holistic, rank-smelling prescription tea of Ancient Chinese Secret nettles, burrs, twigs, fuzzy balls, bark strips, eye of newt, wing of bat. *Nas-tea* we called it, three times a day. It was like someone dug out all the old tupperwares from a bachelor apartment, lined them up, and uncorked each lid. You could see the angry food-spirits sibilantly hissing away, leaving their legacy of *what IS that smell?* Double-boiled and seeped for an hour each time, enough to last for only one day's ration of three cups. Next day, a blink after the noxious smell cleared from the night before, Rinse. Repeat. Retch.

If there is such a thing as retrospect in this case—because I don't remember really *being* there for those fifteen weeks—I find the ambiguities of that semester magically soothing. Having Chris talk me out of tearing my own eyes out every morning because they didn't know how to stay closed—I'd spent all night trying to find out *who the hell's numb-*

---

* Pronounce it as in French—for example, Target becomes "tar-jhay"—therefore, "red poof-e-yay."

nerved, inconsiderable Ass was sitting on the garage door opener, making my garage door eyes stuck, opening and closing, opening and closing. Then going to school, praying that the students could read my mind, that they could time travel to the year before when my passion for writing was actualized in a neat, even-toned, brown-skinned human being. I was hurrying at 8:58 a.m. up the stairs in Adams Humanities to the Third Floor. Then it was 9:50, and I was collecting their homework, glossy-eyeing the roll sheet to make sure I was present, too. For three hours a week, room 3127 was my safe haven, a vacuum of teaching, inspiration, and friendships with no room for morbidity, self-hatred, or ugliness.

There was so little left of me to be alive that semester. I would have given my eyeteeth to have a doctor shove a Benadryl (known as a *Pink* in allergy jargon) the size of a soap bar down my throat. Knock me out, *Bye bye smart Ella*, Chris learned to say when I took prescription-strength Pinks to color up the anti-depressants, the second prescribed anti-itch meds, and the holistic pills, until the better part of Whenever they find a cure for my toxic blood.

Pablo, that class was the fallen light I was fishing for. I didn't know it then, but in my epimethean hindsight, I came to the well needing those drops of light to fill me through to the Next. The problem was, I fell into the well before I could get my act together and fish proper, and these students buoyed me despite myself, me wondering all the while how I was staying afloat.

Diagnoses*

Doctor Ella (*dressed in lab coat as doctor, holding clipboard, reading in a medical tone*)—

1.

It starts off with a few "blue" days where everything that used to stimulate you in any way—food, booze, sex, politics, God—stops. You go numb. You present no affect to any external or internal stimuli short of impulsive narcotic binges. Within two weeks, you are physically unable to wake up. You are sleeping twelve to fifteen hours a day, but it doesn't bother you because you have lost the desire to eat or be awake anyway. After a month of oversleeping, you suddenly stop sleeping altogether.

It's two years later, two years of insomnia and twenty-five pounds of weight gain—of fitful three to four hours of sleep in intervals terrorized by hour-long intervals of suicidal thoughts, manic obsession over absolutely every "why can't" and "why me" possible, and unhindered, gut-wrenching sobbing for no ascertainable reason. You have become house-ridden because of your spontaneous downturns that result in hyperventilating, tears, hot flashes, anger, more tears, and rage. You are afraid to be seen by friends, by strangers, by your own self. You know you need medical help, but you're too miserable to call your regular doctor and ask for a psychiatric referral.

---

* This is from a project in our graduate school program. These individuals I am speaking to are people who have volunteered their hidden illnesses and lives for me to document. I would hang out and talk/pray with them for a couple of hours at a time and then produce something to show them.

Besides, it's not going to help.

**Diagnosis: Clinical Depression (followed by
Anxiety & Panic Disorder)**

2.

Your first diet was at eight years old. Mom—or your primary caregiver, whomever was in the house with you—had to stop giving you your brother's hand-me-downs because even though he's two years older, he's not bigger. You are, and you keep getting. You sense mom is embarrassed by you because she tells you to *try and keep your shirt tucked over your belly, honey* and by the way your brother demands you stop gorging yourself on all the Oreos, *you're supposed to dip the cookies in the milk, not your milk in the cookies!* You get tired of holding your tears at bay, of watching your t-shirt flap over your stomach at recess.

You hear mom's going on a diet. *I want to look good in the black dress I bought for the Christmas party in two weeks,* she coos while scooping cottage cheese into a bowl of canned fruit. You ask if you can do the diet, too, *to look good in my sports jacket for church on Christmas Sunday.* Only, after what you thought was a successful Red Vine and Oreo embargo, along with after-school backyard calisthenics barked at you by big brother, you are standing there in front of the full-length, and the tears can't be held back anymore, because your arms look like unused tubes of toothpaste bulging in their coat sleeves, and now, now your legs are sausage links in the new pair of khakis mom just bought for the special day.

High school. You hide the black circles under your eyes with sunglasses. You're so educated, even elitist about your trips to the bathroom to vomit that you begin conniving your dates so you can take girls to restaurants that have bathrooms far away from general foot traffic, with clean enough stalls for you to bend over. The swim coach has a vague idea that you're being elusive when you take an extra five minutes to make it to roll call from the locker room after school, so he orders a drug test. You pass and everyone else fails, and you become the star freestyle swimmer on the team. The girls are asking you to go study, to the prom, to go steady, to meet their white collar parents. You oblige them, excusing yourself after dinner served on bone china so you can empty out your guilt. The burning in your throat is despicable, but you love that it means you might still fit your jeans tomorrow.

Your popularity begins to suffocate, infringe on your undercover binges and purges. You start to lose sleep over how many pairs of eyes are glued to you through the halls, of how your brother comes home from college skinnier and more fit than ever, and whether mom still thinks you should stuff your shirts into your pants so no one sees your unsightly belly.

On the way to swimming practice, you realize you haven't slept in a month. Your hands start to sweat; you panic. You think the seams are coming undone, that you've been found out, that you'll walk into the locker room and people will start pointing, accusing you of throwing up for no good reason because they can't see you getting any thinner. And they're right. You manage to white knuckle the steering wheel to the first exit where there's an AM/PM Food Mart. There's a dark corner in the empty parking lot behind the school. You drive there, park, take off your sunglasses, and your eyes start to cry involuntarily. See Serotonin deficit. See Depression and Anxiety Disorder.

Diagnosis: Bulimia

3.

In the shower, you find a small lump under your left nipple, size of a pea. No worries, you think, I'm not even 30 years old. Six months and three friend-boys later, the latest companion starts kissing, undoing, coaxing, and petting. He slides his tongue out of your mouth, lines a glistening path down your neck and onto your chest. He cups his lips around your breast, you shiver, and he moves his fingers to pluck at your other nipple, take advantage of your vulnerability. He stops sucking, looks at his hand, still fingering your nipple. The moment squelched. It's now the size of a half dollar, right there, right there, behind the left nipple, just as you found half a year ago.

There are four stages of cancer, One being the earliest, Four also known as End Stage. Your tumor has metastasized, Stage Four, possibly in your lymph nodes, definite spots on your vertebrae. Radical mastectomy on your left breast and all of your nine lymph nodes hooked deep in your arm pit. You can't lift your left arm anymore, *but that's not what you should focus on,* your oncologist warns. You have at least a year of per routine radiation and chemotherapy to endure.

Within the month, you still can't believe how much a person can vomit out every twenty minutes, sometimes for twelve hours straight, until your stomach, throat, and eyes burn. You still can't find the balance of anti-vomit meds to counter the chemo, the chemo has turned your tongue an unnatural gray, made your taste buds hate all your favorite foods so you're sipping broth in between retching. Meanwhile, you are gaining ten, twenty, thirty-five pounds of fluids. Your nerve-deadened left arm starts to swell, get edema, and you have to take four more pills every day just to keep you from being anemic. Soon, the doctor says dryly, *you may start getting blood transfusions on alternate days to your three day a week, two-hour long intravenous chemo sessions.*

You start finding clumps of hair on your pillow, more and more every morning. At the bottom of the shower drain, too, you towel your eyes and look down to see the brown, curly tassels. And your sweet boyfriend, he's determined to support you through this all, while he's trying to love on you, stroke the nape of your neck like you love, he, too, pulls out shaking fingers noosed with your curls. The two of you slump on the couch, he pulls himself off of you quietly, and you stare at your loose shirt, at the vacated place where your breast used to be, wondering just when exactly you stopped being that fickle princess who, on finding a pea under her mattress, made everyone *else* suffer until *she got what she wanted.*

Diagnosis: Inflammatory Breast Cancer

Theology Takes a Hike

What I'm going through is theology hitting the road—wearing flip flops? No. Wearing slippers? Not really. I think of all the dogma I've been inculcated with—all the pretty Bible verses and ethereal promises of death not being final, but merely going to sleep—as having to tie on a pair of cross-country trainers (with enough wiggle room because I hate cramped toes), and hitting the dirt. Walk the talk, or more aptly, walk the thoughts.

Jesus said in John 14 that He was leaving us for a while, but that He would return to take us back to live with Him and God, His father. In a mansion, no doubt—with many rooms, and He wasn't lying (see text). A little while further, He says that He has left us the Holy Spirit to teach us the things He wants us to learn. But a few verses before that, and this I've somehow missed in the way of not even really thinking about it (or believing it for myself), Jesus says that He has given us, his followers, the power and authority to do "even greater things than" He because He is in US, and the Father is in Him.

When a person has end-stage cancer in 2003, this person is the walking dead. With this, is it possible that we, as vessels of God—with Jesus in us and the Holy Spirit's guidance—are able to usher in Amelia's healing? And not just healing spiritually (as in healing vs. curing), but total healing, as in wholeness, as in the definition of HOLY—complete, without stain, and set apart? Because indeed, my last betting dollar is already in someone else's pocket on this, if God heals Amelia's mind, body, and soul completely of any and all cancer—like Jesus did when He was with us, she WILL be set apart for the world to see. *(Can she still be set apart if she dies?)*

And God's glory will be that much more revealed. Who can say her body would have turned around and produced more white fighter cells without any supernatural touch? Amelia, who has to have a blood transfusion regularly because of low hemoglobin. Her body is slowly being vacated of any healthy cells, red or white, while the cancer and the bloating and all the pain meds take charge to terrorize this sinking temple of her body.

I want to see this glory. At the same time, I am fighting with my eyes to keep them fixed on God's FACE and NOT His hand. He is Not about works, and I know this. I know because in the mystery of His existence, He asks us to stay focused on His face, and by doing this, all the other things—those awful, dark, immeasurably painful and consuming things—are worked out and worked away. Not only that, what remains in their place is fullness of joy, restoration, and peace. God's glory means this: He is about love, and love is healing and wholeness.

I understood that only this year while my own demons of sickness and self-hatred were twisting my head away from God's face to see empty hands. What do those empty hands mean? *That He doesn't have anything to give me? Or that He has already given it to me?* That's the danger, that's the ploy of the enemy called the perverted mind. Perverted because I KNOW what truth is—it's God—and I know that He is all-loving, all-powerful, and all-knowing, and that He is pure love, but when my mind gets hold of this empty picture of outpoured hands, it backflips and somersaults into a tailspin, vertigo, then blackout. And in those pits, even when I know there's nowhere else but Up to look, my demented thoughts still weigh down my head, my eyes. Each thought a brick, and brick by brick the wall is built. The light shut out.

What's there but the dank and mold of self-pity, fear, and resolute thoughts of destruction. God has no fellowship with darkness because He is Light, another promise in His Word that has to take a hike. Even there though—according to more of the Word—He never abandons, and all darkness is exposed.

Lord, help me to focus on Your face. Show me how to rig my neck immovable, so that my eyes can only look up. I want to pray Up. I want to look ahead at the path You've laid out, and have the Word be a light unto it while my feet, new in their shoes, learn first to walk steady, and eventually, to run the race set before us.

Dress for Less

She looked down the unadulterated aisles at what seemed like hundreds of thousands of clothes. Once a delight now smothered with impossibility and despair. A worker returned clothes in their general "S," "M," "L" areas, picked up pieces fallen from hangers, forced More into Too Many, like playing an accordion, pushing in from both sides, expelling air.

Suddenly, she forgot what to do. In her natural habitat, she had lost all instinct. Her husband saw her reluctance and immediately reassured her that she could get whatever she wanted. He told her not to worry about the cost, that price wasn't an issue.

Those words, "Get whatever you want," "price is not an issue." How many trips through the years, as she stood at the end of the aisles, filtering out the impulse pieces on the way to the fitting room, getting reprimanded from her roommate that she needed another black skirt like she needed a hole in the head, had she imagined someone saying those liberating lines to her, giving her wings.

Now, she couldn't care less what stylish clothes she was sanctioned to indulge herself in. There wasn't a pair of strappy platforms anywhere on the towering shoe racks to lift her out of this hole.

Today, instead of going to Ross to Dress for Less, she was going to Dress for More. Exactly twenty pounds more from the dietician's assessment. The clinical depression, a monstrous, all-consuming side effect of her disease, kept her from working out, even going out. The year before, her acupuncturist directed her to a holistic physician who told her to eat several tablespoons a day of glorified, nature-packaged cooking oil. *It'll moisturize your internal organs, and eventually bring your skin more moisture than it has,* the doctor said. What it brought her wasn't more moisture, just more skin around the arms, stomach, legs, and face to be sick—bulging uncomfortably in her old Ross shirts, skirts, and pants. Still cracking, still red, still bleeding.

There was something so utterly catastrophic about *having to shop* versus *wanting to shop*.

She excused herself from her husband, pretending she was excited to look at the Ladies' section. He should go upstairs and browse in the Men's, she told him. Going up the escalator, she smiled at his wink, using all her energy to sustain the corners of her mouth until his ascent was complete. She talked herself into looking at the larger sizes, trying to convince herself they were the same clothes, would make her feel just as pretty, just as *normal*, but more *comfortable*—for now. A handful of recalibrated-for-her shirts, skirts, pants, even underwear in her hands, she met her husband at the fitting room entrance. He complimented her choices, saying she should definitely go back and get them in other colors if she wanted.

In the fitting room, she crumpled to tears, burying her head in the clothes pile, sitting down on the bench corner, using her knees to keep her face from falling off. She pushed her wet, stinging cheek next to the mirror. After a few minutes, she wiped off, reapplied the greasy medicinal ointment that streaked, and waited to calm down.

She thanked the fitting room attendant, quietly handing her the clothes, regretting that she didn't fit any of them this time. She kissed the back of her husband's hand as they left, telling him *this* Ross must not have had a good shipment. He promised to drive her to another Ross across town the next day. *If she wanted.* She said maybe and that they'd better get home to make her holistic tea.

It was the first time she left empty-handed.

Tofu Meatloaf?

1 cup hot water
1 tablespoon Vegex
2 cloves garlic, minced
1 teaspoon Italian seasoning
1 teaspoon paprika
1 teaspoon salt
1 pound soft tofu, mashed
1 cup dry whole wheat bread crumbs
1 cup rolled oats
1 cup finely chopped pecans
1 large onion, chopped
¼ cup gluten flour

Dissolve Vegex in hot water. Stir in garlic and seasonings.

Mix remaining ingredients together. Add Vegex mixture and mix well (it will be stiff). Place in a sprayed 1½ quart casserole dish and bake uncovered at 375 degrees F for 1 hour or until set in the middle. Will hold its shape if turned out on a platter.

Garnish with cherry tomatoes and parsley. Serves 10.

Per ¹⁄₁₀ loaf (½ cup): 203 calories; 10.5 g. protein (20%); 19.5 g. carbohydrate (36%); 10.5 g. fat (44%); 390 mg. sodium; 97 mg. calcium; 0 mg. cholesterol.

I crossed the street while the oven was heating, wondering if I could get away with making the fake meatloaf without the right-sized casserole dish. At the store, I got the paprika, *what does this stuff do for meatloaf anyway?* and waited in line to pay. I started to chuckle to myself, half nervous, half in disbelief. I was trying to make fake meatloaf for my girlfriends, a whole room full of them, for the first time, and they all ate *normal* food. What would they think of me?

"Vegan, what's that again?" I could hear them asking at different times in the night. I would tell them how meat and dairy are taboo for us because of my health, and to help explain it, I'd show them the picture of the vegan food pyramid, pointing out where fruits, vegetables, nuts, and legumes replace the meat and dairy blocks in the triangle.

If they got really interested, I would break out the books and lecture notes from my stay at Weimar. I'd explain to them how it is a residential medical facility where they basically detoxed my body for three weeks. The MDs and PhDs lectured three or four times a day about how harmful animal products are to our bodies, *especially* ours—the patients there—because we were already sick and more sensitive to what we put in our systems.

Back at the apartment, I measured out the paprika and spooned it into the bowl. I balled up the un-meatloaf and spread it out on the only baking sheet we had. In the back of my mind, I started organizing my day so I could fit in a quick trip to the co-op and buy ready-made food if this stuff tasted like the bottom of my shoe.

I had an hour before I could fork it and see if it still *whinnied* or *moo-ed* or, I suppose, *oatmeeealed*, so I tried to put the mail away. There was a letter from Weimar, from the pastor this time, reminding me to trust in God, to do my breathing exercises while I walked my five miles a day, and asking me if I finished writing my Yosemite story for him. He was a regular contributor to a recently-started magazine called *Creation Illustrated*. Inside were articles by scientists and people of faith alike, all trying to explain through nature, through biblical texts, and through personal experience their observations of nature. He gave me a copy of the magazine wherein he had written an article about how grafting white and red flowers to make pink ones brought him closer to understanding how fascinating nature, and by extension, the Creator was. Pastor thought my trip to Yosemite would be a story from which the editor could draw a poignant demonstration of, "Someone out there watching over us."

I turned on the computer, determined to try and honor my obligation to him. And after all, it could be a publication under my belt! As I began to write through an introduction to ease myself into detailing the Fall, I realized the only work I had to do was physically push the "On" button and sit myself in front of the screen. This story is one I've told so many times, it had begun to tell itself. If anyone asked me what the most amazing thing is that has ever happened in my life, hands down this was it.

After an unplanned retrospective of the entire waterFall, the symphony of fireworks exploding around all the flashbacks of lifelong lessons I learned suddenly stopped their hoorah-for-me chorus. Looking over what my fingers had pounded into the computer's keyboard, phrases like, "had I not fallen...I might have missed the most important point..." and "I was chosen to go through this valley for a much bigger purpose..." gave me the nauseating feeling that I was deviating from the magazine's objective that I originally set out to meet. The nature part was somewhere in there, but the packaging was verging on sentimental drivel, trying to force a nice Spielbergian ending, tying up all the loose ends, sure to make for a blockbuster. You'd think by now, seven years later, significantly in response to 9-11, I would've started to really believe not everything needs to be an opportunity to be didactic. There are some times in life where, when things like this happen, my reaction—both immediate and long term—could only be, *That's shitty, just shitty.*

I didn't have the time to, how should I say, *introspect* through this. My fakeloaf was getting bored cooking. By the time I shut down the computer, I had left it in for almost an hour and a half. If my girlfriends complained it was too dry, I'd tell them I was watching out for them, that I didn't want them to get salmonella from undone tofu and, God forbid, raw bread crumbs.

When I looked in the oven, it looked like I was cooking one large, 16 x 12 inch piece of beef(like) jerky. I took a fork and, shaking my head, tugged off the corner. It crunched just right in my mouth. The flavors blended together well (all hail paprika!); it was a saltlick just tasty enough to satiate the most PMSing of us all.

I soon realized meatloaf shouldn't crunch, so I took a knife to the hardened frame of the loaf and pared it down. I wanted to keep up the façade for this first time feeding vegan propaganda to my closest girlfriends, make them look at the suspicious meatloaf and at least, if all else

failed, recognize what it was *supposed* to be. I cut the flat loaf into serv-
ing-sized rectangles and flowered them on the most distractingly pretty
platter I had. I cut tomatoes into little florets as garnish and laid them
out in mini-bunches on leaves of lettuce in strategic places throughout
the presentation.

When the doorbell rang, I was so engrossed in my transformation
I forgot there was a reason I was dressing up food. Theresa and May
came in, *hug hug kisses on cheeks*. Theresa held up a plastic bag with
Soy Dreams ice cream and Trader Joe's Vegan Chocolate Chip Cookies in it—the only brands that resemble the real foods enough to be
satisfied—and headed straight for the kitchen.

"You didn't have to do that, Theresa. I feel bad. Did you have to look
up stores with vegan dessert alternatives?"

"Yeah, but that's okay." She was looking for room in the freezer. "One
of my coworkers is lactose intolerant and told me where to find ice cream
she could eat. I found these cookies there, too. Have you had them? They
look normal. They should be good!"

I made room for the ice cream in the freezer, took out a small plate
for the cookies. May was giving herself permission to sit down on the
couch and take the load off of her long day teaching middle school. I
could see her breathing deeply, stretching her arms out, sighing into the
cushions.

"I have tasted that brand, and yes, they taste *normal*," I offered, grateful for her effort. So that I wouldn't expect too much from my guests,
I had bought Breyer's ice cream and fresh-baked cookies from Costco
the day before. In case they weren't ready to learn to walk after crawling
through a vegan main dish, I thought this would help them forget their
sacrifice on my dietary behalf.

"Yummm. Something smells SO delicious! What did you cook us for
dinner?!"

May got up from the couch, bee-lined to the platter I was bringing out to the dinner table, bent over and whiffed hard. "Meatloaf! I
haven't had that in YEARS! My mom used to cook us meatloaf on cold

days—just like tonight! Oh man, this is going to be wonderful. All the comforts I miss!"

Theresa clapped her hands. "Meatloaf? No kidding?! Me, too. You're going to have to give me the recipe for this. I'm always looking for new things to cook. Wanna give me cooking lessons?"

I hoped they didn't see my eyes widen until they pushed my eyebrows off my face. I turned to the kitchen laughing, once again, in disbelief. They didn't fool me. These girls loved me through the last year of sickness, praying for me while I was in rehab, sending me e-mails and phone cards to keep in touch with Chris because he had to work to pay for the treatment and could only visit on the weekends. Even though we had only been married for two months before I took leave. They knew I was abruptly reprogrammed and could never eat, live, or breathe the same way again.

Getting from point A to point B with highlighted episodes of anxiety attacks, clinical depression, severe insomnia, fits of rage, not to mention the physical symptoms of my disease. Now *that was shitty.*

They knew this wasn't real meatloaf, that they walked in here bound by an unwritten contract that they might have to feast on salad and both kinds (real and fake) of ice cream and cookies as they pushed their mealy-loaves around to the edges of their plates. That I might whip out the recipe and impose it on them, and they would go home remembering *not* to cook this dish because it tasted shy of meatloaf, closer to penny loafers. *Remember that time when Ella cooked us meatloafers for dinner?!*

The other girls came in intervals, the last of them bringing a twin bag of vegan chocolate chip cookies from Trader Joe's. As we sat down to eat, one of the girls was staring at my foot. She touched the scars on both sides of my ankle, and asked me again to tell her the Story of my fall. She loved hearing it, as did the others. They tell me somehow it's a distraction from their tunnel-visioned, microscopic lives, reminding them that there's something bigger out there. Their favorite part is when the paramedics rappelled out of the helicopter like Rambo. Mine, too, for obvious reasons.

These girls I call sisters when talking about them outside of our circle, chewed and smiled, smiled and crunched, listening to me recite my story again, telling me about their weeks, making me laugh at their funny faces until I believed they *really did* like my meatloaf, and that this meal might be the next most amazing thing, hands down, that's ever happened to me.

Fieldwork

Pressing On

From: decastro <decastro@rohan.sdsu.edu>
To: <adavis@hotmail.com>, <eckh@aol.com>,
<adriennelyton@yahoo.com>, <pattibis@aol.com>,
"babez in Christ" <babezinchrist@yahoogroups.com>,
<eppl@cox.net>, <jamiehf@yahoo.com>,
<ssully@yahoo.com>, <jules@aol.com>,
<stylish@hotmail.com>, <jbennet03@sbcglobal.net>,
<kaoruinteriors@san.rr.com>
CC: <jcelestial@san.rr.com>
Date: Tue, October 14, 2003 11:06 pm
Subject: Amelia is in the Hospital

Hello sisters,

Chris and I returned home tonight to hear a phone message that our
sister, Amelia, was taken to the hospital tonight because the pain in her
kidneys was unbearable. Last week, they did a CatScan because Amelia
was having swelling in her abdomen. Her doctor doesn't tell her details
anymore b/c she doesn't want/need to hear them, so his words last
Friday over the phone were, "the disease is progressing."

Amelia's cancer is now affecting all of her major organs in some way--
she has fluid in her lungs and around her heart, there are "spots" on her
liver, her right kidney is giving her a lot of pain, and there is some kind
of block in her bladder/ureter.

The original plan to do a noninvasive procedure in a week and a half to
relieve some of the swelling is now changed. BY TOMORROW MORNING
(Wednesday--today when you read this), she and husband Dane have to
decide which of two proposed invasive surgical procedures Amelia will
go through. Both of them have the goal of relieving the pain in her right
kidney, and both are equally invasive.

Dane asks us to spread the prayer request to everyone who can pray
for their decision-making to be the "right one for Amelia". At this point,

what they really want is "God to come and save her in the eleventh hour" without the need for surgery.

We do not give up faith that God can do any and all things, so we ultimately hope for TOTAL healing of her mind, body, and soul. Today, we also need your prayers in faith that God will show the Button family what procedure they should agree to for Amelia's pain to be alleviated.

Of course, continued prayer of protection over Amelia, Dane, and little Emily's hearts is coveted. Let's ask God in confidence to keep fear from entering this family's domain.

If any of you ladies were planning on bringing the Buttons a meal in the next week or so, please hold off until we know when Amelia is coming home. If we find that Dane and Emily could use food while they are supporting Amelia at the hospital, I will let you know.

If you are led, please ask for prayer from any other warriors who can stand in the gap, intercede, and lower Amelia down through the roof at Jesus' feet during this difficult time.

Trusting the Father completely,
On our knees,
~Ella

℃⁄౩

I went to work the next day and arranged my schedule for the next few days. I took off all day of work on Thursday so I could devote any time helping Dane and Amelia with any little details and also so I could do my shift of friendship and prayer with Amelia. I asked everyone else in other praying communities I'm connected to to pray.

Next morning, Wednesday, I went to work secretly relieved that it was my last day of the workweek. I would get to spend the rest of the week being with Amelia and learning more about loving her, helping her to record this rough patch in her struggle, and hoping with her. Before Spanish class, I retrieved my messages from our home phone. I think it was out of reflex because just a week and a half before, I had to do this—check my cell and home answering services to see if I was going to be a proud new good friend-auntie to newborn twins. (Hope had her twins the week before, and she was home trying to learn the double football hold and nurse both Elias and Sofia at the same time!)

Eunice, one of the women we met with every Friday, left a message. "Ella," she said with a small weight in her throat, "this is Eunice. I'm calling because we heard more news about Amelia. It is not good. She is in a lot more pain, in and out of consciousness. The doctors say from a human standpoint, she only has a few days."

I sat down in the mentor office and took off my backpack.

From: decastro <decastro@rohan.sdsu.edu>
To: <dmaglk@cox.net>
Date: Wed, October 15, 2003 2:07 pm
Subject: Missing Class--Amelia

Hi Professor,

I am headed to the hospital right now to be with Amelia. Things have taken a turn in the last two weeks, the pain has put her in the hospital, and now the doctors are saying "from a human standpoint, she only has a few days."

I hope to return to class next week. Feel free to express this news to the class; we can use all the support possible.

peace.
~Ella

ℰℱ

I thought of e-mailing my Spanish instructor to say I was going to miss class today, but I forgot. My coworkers worked quietly around me, obviously understanding that something serious was happening in our small office space. I got out my address book and started to call our other friends to pray—an e-mail was out of the question at this point. Although it was the most efficient way to organize everything all these months, it felt like things had quickly gotten too personal for the neat, binary confines. In the middle of my calls, in my desperation to reach someone besides an answering machine, I did write an e-mail to one of the women's prayer groups that both Amelia and I were part of.

After some messages were left, Kristine called back from the hospital. She couldn't reach my cell because it wasn't working, so she called Chris' cell and he called me at work. She had been with Amelia all morning. She said Amelia wanted to see me and to come right away. Kristine would then get to go home and take her four home-schooled daughters to their ballet lessons.

On the way to Kaiser, I challenged myself to really, really admit if I was afraid that Amelia was going to die. I assumed it would come out—that this incredulity at her sudden downturn would become skepticism in my belief that God was going to heal her—but nothing of the sort came out. I was on the other side of that valley. I surprised myself at how unwavering I felt. I turned onto Mission Gorge Road believing just the same during all those months that if it was God's will, He would heal Amelia's physical body from the cancer.

I parked at the backside lot of Zion's parking lot. This was the Kaiser hospital I went to for my prescriptions and appointments. I took Amelia here for her first chemo session with her latest drug, Gemcitabine. She pronounced it as I read the bag, gem-sight-a-bean. The second time I heard that was at the American Cancer Society's Breast Cancer Walk kick-off breakfast a couple of months later. It was one of the three newest drugs available in 2003.

Dane hugged, pulled me outside the hospital door. He said that this morning, Amelia's doctor asked him to consider not doing the procedure to relieve stress in her bladder because there was so much cancer in her bladder. He wanted Dane to authorize them to make Amelia as "comfortable as possible" for the next few days. Dane was hard, didn't want to give in. He said all of her three sisters and mom were getting on planes from the East Coast to see her, and he was trying to get her some relief so she could wait for them in the next day and a half.

I asked Dane how Amelia was when she woke up that morning. He said after the doctor talked to them, she said, "I'm dying." She'd never said that before.

I assured Dane I could be the first one to stay overnight with her so that Kristine wouldn't have to come back that night. She could take the morning shift the next day. We were going to ask Eunice to come for some of the time. Dane didn't want Amelia to be left alone, without other Christians whom she could pray with, especially when he needed to leave to take a nap and spend time with Emily. He tried to tell me that Amelia needed help to get up and use the commode, that there was a way she needed to be lifted off of the bed. He was a little nervous, but I told him immediately that I had grown up in hospitals my whole life—all of my cousins and my mom and sister work in hospitals—and I was not squeamish at all.

We walked into the hospital room. A woman with mouse-brown hair and a look of trepidation to match sat in the corner of the room, glossy-eyed behind her thick glasses. Dane introduced me to her, his sister.

By that point, Amelia was no longer talking. Her eyes were dilated so large, her usually blue eyes looked completely black. She did not look like Amelia, not the woman we prayed and laughed with nonchalantly five days earlier for the last Friday prayer meeting. She had gained twenty pounds from four bags of pain meds draining intravenously into her. She looked so large and bulbous—I kept thinking she didn't look like a human anymore. She struggled to lift her head up as it would fall in her delirium. She was like a dying animal: moaning, confused, unable to articulate anything it felt.

Dane said she could hear us and respond, but that she was too out of it to speak. They were giving her so much medication to prepare her for a form of a colonoscopy that he ordered, against the doctor's recommendation, to try one more time to put a tube in her to relieve some of the fluid that was stopped up in her bladder. By that morning, she was only able to urinate small amounts of blood.

I moved to her side and stroked her arms, then her legs. Dane was going to tell her I was there, but I shh-shhd him because I didn't want her to feel any obligation. She was always trying to think of the other person. Her coworker from the foster care shelter, Klea, came in and her face dropped. She stood across from me and held Amelia from the other side. We shook hands over Amelia and introduced ourselves.

"Oh yes, Ella. I've heard so many wonderful things about you."

When she said her name, I said I had heard even greater things about her from Amelia. Klea was the one Amelia would call to come and pick up Emily to stay with her during the long nights and hospital E.R. trips.

She was the other person who shopped and helped to clean their house while I organized other people from our church to do the same from our end.

Klea told me how, when she left two hours before to do some errands, Amelia was completely cognizant, calm, breathing well. Now, she struggled to gasp short breaths, and she was so groggy she could not open her eyes or mouth to say anything. Klea quietly whispered to me as we held Amelia's hands that she seemed to have taken a drastic nosedive in the last two hours.

There were a lot of tears. I stood at Amelia's side and prayed. Words pissed me off. There seemed no time for articulation and plea bargaining. All I could do was repeat "Jesus" over and over. I could see Klea looking a little curiously at me through her tears. The nurses filtered in and out, all of them Filipino. It was more than a small comfort to lock eyes with them, have them nod at me that I was doing a nice thing standing there, and they even stopped and prayed with me for a few seconds when I would begin again to say Jesus' name.

Dane sat at Amelia's feet, head in hands, nervous. The World Series was on TV; he looked at the score now and again.

Amelia's breathing got shorter, and she began to fuss and swing her arms languidly around her face, trying to take off her oxygen mask it seemed. We moved around to let Dane get closer to Amelia. I felt both honored and inconsiderate, out of place, being there. I had only known Amelia during her sickness, and here was her husband, the man she'd been with for fourteen years, smoothing her hair and whispering how much he loved her into her ear. And at the end of the bed, arms crossed, tears blurring her face, was Klea—Amelia's best friend in San Diego for the nine years they worked together. Klea had more right to be there than me. Even Dane's sister who could not get up from her hunched position on the chair knew more about Amelia and somehow deserved to be there more than myself.

Dane asked Amelia to squeeze his hand if she wanted him to go home and get Emily. Emily was at her daycare, and she could come and sit with her mom one more time. Amelia did not squeeze. He asked several times. He asked me or Klea to get some blank paper and crayons from the nurses. He traced Amelia's right hand with each of the three dry erase markers the nurse gave Klea.

I moved to the chair next to Amelia, continuing to pray for mercy. At that point, I wanted the pain to stop. I had a tangible moment of lostness, of not feeling God's presence in the least. I asked Him as I alternated between sitting and standing at her side if He would show me He was there. "I need to see you, Jesus," I remember pleading, "because I've never been to this place and I need to know You're real."

Dane walked away to talk to the nurses outside I think, ask when the stronger pain meds were coming from downstairs. Klea and I were holding both of her hands, and she began to pull both of them away. It was as if she was trying to sit up, then stand up. She was amazingly strong—I had scratch marks all over my hands and arms from trying to calm her down. Klea and I asked her what she needed, and she continued to pull off her oxygen, yank off her headband, and move from side to side trying to use the guard rails to get up. Clearly, she was too weak and full of so much liquid to stand, but she was determined nonetheless.

We asked her again what she needed, that we would get it. She mumbled and moaned, and then as plain as if she was talking on the phone or sitting at her work desk she said in one breath, "I need to make sure everything's taken care of."

Klea and I reassured her profusely, attempting to comfort her in a chorus, crying and confident at once. *Honey, everything's alright. Emily's fine, Dane's fine, we're all fine. Don't worry about anything; it's all taken care of. You just relax now. Everything's fine.*

By this time, Dane walked back in and Klea moved him into her spot and pulled a chair up for him. Dane sat across from me, still stroking Amelia's face and whispering prayers to God in her ear. Klea's dark spiky hair and flashes of silver rings on all her fingers came at my peripheral vision as she paced the foot of the bed. Dane's sister, tacit, did not move.

Amelia began being restless again. She tried to pull herself up by the guard rails, and we kept asking her what she wanted, and that she shouldn't try to get up. "Just rest, Amelia," we said, "It's okay." Dane seemed to recognize Amelia's behavior of discomfort, most likely from taking care of her in bed during the especially painful days at home. He started pulling pillows from around the room, from the recliner he had slept in the night before. He asked us to get one of the nurses, and together, they lifted Amelia up by the arms and shoulders and put several pillows behind her. Dane thought she wanted to sit up. It seemed to help because her shallow breathing relaxed a bit, and she was able to draw slightly deeper breaths. After another several minutes, Amelia began shifting listlessly around again, so Dane had the nurse elevate her bed until she was sitting completely upright. She stopped fussing at that point, and we could let go of her arms and breathed steadier along with her.

Again, I asked Jesus to show up.

Dane sat back down at her side and began to kiss Amelia all over her face. Soon, his earnestness in begging God to heal his wife shifted. Instead, he simply told Amelia as he kissed her, "I love you, I love you so much, I love you."

The three of us women there began to weep louder, and this time I felt the peace I was asking for. Jesus had shown up through her husband—no more expecting or asking, just giving. As I watched their intimacy, I knew Amelia needed to hear this.

After another hour of watching and praying in and out of tears, Amelia's closest Aunt Amy walked in. She looked like Amelia's blend of Chinese and Caucasion—light skin, dark hair, eyes at a slight slant. Dane told Amelia her aunt was there, and Amy came to Amelia's side.

She told Amelia all of the memories she had of Amelia. "You were always the golden child," she said, "You never did anything the easy way, did you?" She said, "All of your family, our family, will be here in the morning for a reunion. We can't wait to be with you."

Aunt Amy's sincerity pulled more grief out of all of us. We cried in rounds, failing to be quiet in case Amelia still could hear us. It was a good-bye talk, a patronizing, soothing farewell to her niece. Amelia suddenly pulled her hand out of her Aunt Amy's. I thought that she might have no longer had any energy left after all she did before we sat her up. The nurses had increased the medications dripping into her from the four intravenous bags to the highest dose allowed for the hour. She seemed, again, persistent to either get up or to do something with her hand. As she pulled her hand aggressively away from her aunt, her arm flew up, straight into the air, and fell, eventually resting her hand behind her head. It looked a little anachronistic, as if the time for Amelia to put her hand behind her head and relax was long gone. I smiled, a small one, and imagined Amelia sitting on a hammock anywhere but in a hospital room.

I looked around the room—there was one of us from each sphere of Amelia's world—her husband and his sister, Klea from work, myself from her church family, and now her aunt by her side.

Twenty minutes later, Amelia's breathing changed from spastic, short breaths to slightly deeper breaths. Her upright position might have helped her breathing; maybe the fluid building in her lungs was alleviated. Aunt Amy held Amelia's right hand; I was next to her stroking Amelia's leg; Klea at the foot of the bed, Dane's sister still in the chair, immobile; and Dane at Amelia's left side.

He thanked her for the beautiful daughter she gave him, and he thanked Jesus out loud for Amelia's gift of life to him. He was struggling to see Amelia like this, in so much discomfort, unable to express herself in any way by this point. He kept begging Jesus to "take the pain away, to send comfort, to send His Spirit to do it." Anything, he said, he'd take anything not to see her in this pain.

After some quiet, Dane kissed his wife's lips. I could see his dark, wavy hair linger in front of her face. Behind closed mouth and wide-open eyes, I asked Jesus for mercy; I asked Him if He could take her.

Dane looked at Amelia and told her, with confidence and sincerity, "You can go to Jesus now. Go to Him. That's where the pain will stop. Don't worry about me and Emily. He has us, and He'll never leave us. You just go. You can go."

I looked down, away, again feeling intrusive during this most intimate time, wondering again why I was allowed, or more specifically, chosen to be one of the five who would watch this.

Within a few minutes, Amelia breathed a few deeper, slower, more peaceful breaths. I watched in awe, knowing after her last that she had stopped breathing, but I didn't have the guts to walk over to Dane and tell him I thought she was gone. Another minute passed before he looked up from thanking God for everything, praying over her, and he told me to get the nurse.

After she checked Amelia's vitals, she got a flashlight and made sure Amelia's pupils were unresponsive. She closed Amelia's eyes and patted her hair, nodded to us and said she had passed. She lowered the bed and laid her hand on a few of us before leaving and closing the door. Klea and I walked over to Dane and put our arms around him from behind. He was suspended over Amelia in a moment of disbelief.

His burst into hysterics wasn't long-lived, or maybe not as long as I wanted it to be to help me express my own shock and grief over what we just witnessed. He sobbed uncontrollably until Klea held him, shaking him and saying in his ear, "It's okay Dane. She's in a better place. She doesn't feel any more pain." I almost wanted to tell her not to do that, to let Dane have as much of it out as he could, but I also knew Klea might not have wanted to see Dane hurting so openly because she was scared of what she might have to feel, too.

We waited outside, everyone on cell phones making the preliminary calls. I didn't have my phone—still broken—so I sat and made lists of who I'd have to call when I got home. The network of people praying around San Diego was lengthy. We would have to do a phone tree.

I went home in a fog—the fog I suppose that happens. I recalled seeing Amelia the moment her spirit left her body. It was true—it was not Amelia anymore. What remained was a shell, a tent, a vacated place where she used to live. Walking into the house, Chris was sitting in the dusk's light, waiting for news.

"Everyone's been calling," he said. "They're all driving right now to go to the hospital to pray, or whatever." He pulled me into a hug. "They want to know what they can do. I told them to keep praying until you could tell them more."

୧∕୬

From: "Anna Davis" <adavis@hotmail.com>
To: "decastro" <decastro@rohan.sdsu.edu>
Date: Wed, October 15, 2003 10:20 pm
Subject: No turning back

Dearest Ella,

How are doing, dear sister? I still have a lot of questions to God that go through my mind -I DO NOT UNDERSTAND HIS WAYS!!!! But I do know that I know He is GOD, He is who He says He is, He is still Holy and Sovereign, Jesus Christ is full of love, grace, and mercy, our God - our Father is bigger than the air we breathe - He is faithful...and when you said talking about your thesis "there is no turning back", it was like a church bell rang inside of me...There is no turning back, dear Ella, we need to press on, we need to keep praying for others, we need to keep loving Jesus and His people and keep praying for them: for healing, restoration, provision, etc...just keep praying knowing that God is faithful...do not give up...

୧∕୬

For some reason, this portion of Anna's e-mail—among many e-mails sent to me over the next few days—took precedence. I wasn't in the state of giving up, I was more determined than ever to push on, to press on. There's a verse in the Bible that says, "Let us acknowledge the LORD; let us press on to acknowledge him. As surely as the sun rises, he will appear; he will come to us like the winter rains, like the spring rains that water the earth." That was in my head. If I was going to go through the natural stages of grief and give up, or simply stop in my tracks to be pissed off, all that stuff, I wasn't anywhere near there. I was in shock still—I had never watched someone die. I knew the stages of grief were inevitable, are inevitable (are happening now), and I was numb to this e-mail (to all of them really). Still, it rang as some kind of banner over me, a sort of prophecy that I would return to later. Surely, through this experience, my faith would come out more refined than ever; it surprised and yet

sated me that this was the first time in my different experiences of trag-
edies that me leaving my faith was not an option.

I packed some hiking clothes, some art supplies, and I told Chris I
thought we should still go to the church leadership retreat in Idyllwild
planned long ago for that weekend, if for nothing else, to get away with
some of the people in this family of believers so we could do some safe
mourning alongside each other.

℅

From: decastro <decastro@rohan.sdsu.edu>
To: <jules@aol.com>
CC: <lauren@lhsn.com>, <Eunice@eunicers.com>
Date: Sat, October 18, 2003 4:57 pm
Subject: About Amelia and her Memorial Service

Hello sisters,

(Julie, can you please forward this to the women's group?)

I just returned from a retreat for the Coast Vineyard leaders. I only went
because I knew God could heal some of our pain in the company of
friends, and that's what happened. Anna and I were there, and we were
fortunate enough to be blessed by being two of the ladies who prayed
every Friday for Amelia. It was especially difficult for us--we felt totally
poured out and tired. There was a lot of crying, all the time throughout
worship and whenever we remembered our Amelia.

The good news is that as I thought about Amelia and how I missed her, I
didn't miss her more than I wanted her to be with Jesus. In fact, it made
me hunger to be with the Lord myself. I want the kingdom to come!

A common vision that swept through Dwight, Anna's husband, during
this weekend, is of our church being in a boat. And we were called to
stop steering it and pull off the rudder and let God take us where He
wills on the river. During the second night when I completely broke,
God showed me more. He wanted us all to jump out of the boat, to hear
Jesus say, "Come", and to walk on water. He had me asking those leaders
to partner with me, to hold me up, and to do this kind of work with me
because I can't do it by myself. The grief is too heavy.

The next morning (today), Dwight saw the boat transform into a raft,
and it was headed over the falls. He said in a situation like that, the raft
guide calls out, "EVERYONE TO THE LEFT" or "EVERYONE TO THE RIGHT",

and everyone leaves the raft. If it flips over and doesn't clear the falls, it gets destroyed. And We're in a place where we're being called to go left and right, to leave the raft and all of our safety nets into a place of deeper, more risky ministry to find those people who, like Amelia, are drowning in pain, sin, and loneliness.

I left this retreat renewed and determined. The feeling I had all weekend was that I felt so tired, but not in an exhausted way. I felt more like I was completely poured out--I've never put so much of myself into any one person or thing. The beautiful part is that it felt "natural," like this is what I was created to do: I want to bring God's love to the despairing, to the weak, to the lost and hungry. Anna and I held each other and reconfirmed that even though we are confused and in grief, there is Hope. We are committed more than ever to healing in Jesus' name.

(I went off just then--but I couldn't hold it in!)

Amelia's Memorial Service will be this Tuesday at 6 p.m. at Coast Vineyard.

In addition, there is a request for specific names of people who can donate time and/or money to help Amelia's family with food during the week, bills/expenses, and other needs as they arise. Klea, one of Amelia's closest friends who has been Emily's babysitter during every long night in the hospital, is organizing this. I will work with her to construct this list. Even a one time gift of love will not be unappreciated.

Please spread the word about the Memorial Service. Klea is also having a reception at her house in Chula Vista after the service for those who can come.

Pressing On,
~Ella

❧

The lights of Springall Academy's gymnasium are off. Candles of all shapes and sizes dimly, solemnly light the austere space instead. More than the one hundred chairs are full within minutes. Instead of half of the gym used, as anticipated, the entire gym is quickly packed with people, grabbing chairs from stacks at the back wall. Large, wild bunches flowers loosed in baskets, not vases—the way Amelia loved them, the way she designed them at her own wedding—proud shades of pink roses, bold and tender white lilies, earthy greens to cushion the flowers' personalities. The two creative scrapbooks that Amelia made—one for each year of her daughter's life—propped on the white-linen-draped table next to the Guest Book. There is a crystal bowl full of different-shaped gold buttons, a sign next to them welcoming people to take the buttons. "Place these buttons wherever you can easily see them. Remember to pray for the Button family when you see them."

A merging of communities floods the gymnasium. There are all of her co-workers, clutching for life onto their spouses or each other, shaken with grief. There is her supervisor who can't stop talking past the requested five minutes; she can't stop praising how many of the kids' lives Amelia literally saved from suicide and their abusive situations. She remembers how Amelia knew no boundaries—she loved to love the kids, especially at Christmas—her office with no sitting or desk space because "every kid *had* to have the same exact presents in each of their stuffed stockings!" Her best friend, who grew up with her on the East Coast, regrets the time she didn't spend with Amelia these last two years. She acknowledges that, "I have to reconcile this—all of us will have to—for peace of mind." There are young people—barely grown into their growing bodies—in awkwardly loose dress shirts and ties. A few of them look both deeply saddened and profoundly confused. I just know that these are the kids Amelia's saved.

It seems as if the tribes, tongues, and nations are here to remember Amelia.

I had spent all day throwing away attempts to say what I know Amelia would have wanted me to say. I didn't want there to be any cause for ambiguity. Especially towards the end of her life, Amelia's life was a testimony where, in addition to showing us all that she went through, there was a need to simply tell what I saw. After I look at Chris for a look of support, I go up to the podium, sheets of paper rolled in my hand.

Amelia's Memorial Service, 21 October 2003

It's strange, standing here. I had dreamt of a day like this, when I would get to read to a group of people. I would share a handful of brilliant pages full of stunning insights into Life and Living as seen through Amelia's battle and victory over breast cancer. My mom would be there to hear parts of my final thesis project—this book length creative work that I called *Amelia—No Turning Back*. Along with everyone else in the audience, my mom would see how her own recently-diagnosed breast cancer can be cured because of all the hope and light on those pages. And there would be Amelia, sitting in the second row, at the end of the aisle—in case Emily got too feisty or because she might squirt her juice box into Amelia's face—quietly celebrating all the healing! After my reading and applause, the Q & A time would bring the most anticipated question: *So, what happened to Amelia, the woman you wrote about this past year and a half?* Amelia and I said that's when we would look at each other and smile, and she would come up and sit next to me on the little café stage, wave her hand and tell everyone, "Hi, I'm Amelia. If any of you want to talk to me about how I was saved from this disease, I would love to share with you my source of life." We even talked jokingly about how I could put her address at the end of my book so people could always keep in touch with her as she approached 65, 70 years old, still, in her famous words, "as *fabulous* as ever."

Obviously, these plans were not exactly what happened. Today, I stand here after pages and paragraphs of half-finished starts, trying to write the most authentic, worthy pages I could about her journey. I was fortunate to be called into helping to lead the Women's Ministry at our church shortly after I, myself was healed of an all-consuming genetic disease. That's when I got to see through my own God-redeemed eyes how much He loved Amelia, too.

I truly first connected with Amelia when I spent a weekend at a Healing Conference in La Jolla. Not knowing what to expect (but hoping for everything), Amelia and I spent session after session taking notes, debriefing the talks by healing pastors, and chatting about house decorating, esp. "Trading Spaces" (ahh, the instant bond). I told Amelia that somehow, when she first walked into church months before in her cute straw hat, I felt like I wanted to be in her life, and she in mine. She told me quietly that she felt the same way after the few times we'd talked, but she was scared that I wouldn't want to be her friend. She said she thought it would be hard for our community to want to be friends with someone who might die. I hadn't even thought of that, so I grabbed her hand and I told her, "*But Amelia, this is a forever sisterhood.*"

After that meeting, we both started day-dreaming about traveling together with another girlfriend who also has victory over sickness, speaking, encouraging and bringing God's healing to men, women, and children across this "funny blue marble." Our relationship grew more deeply as we organized weekly Friday afternoon prayer meetings focused on loving Amelia with Jesus' love, listening to her real, difficult questions without judgment, and asking for healing on her behalf. As I looked through my two journals full of notes I had taken of these gatherings, I saw pearls that Amelia herself had asked me to help her remember as part of her own healing, and eventually as part of her vision to serve other suffering, sick individuals. I want to share some of these gifts from Amelia because in obedience to her and God's will, this was the main reason she invited me to write about her life.

Amelia was fiercely candid with her emotions. By doing this, she showed me how to worship God in spirit and in truth. In over twenty group meetings of prayer with other women all across San Diego and the country, what I noted was how each time, what we prayed for and heard from the Lord were promises given and fulfilled through the Bible. So many of her own Psalms came pouring out of Amelia's mouth. She was completely vulnerable, pouring out her heart, her anguish, and at the same time, *choosing* to have faith in God because she trusted Him. The psalmists did not spew out vague, passionless, religious clichés. Like they did over and over, Amelia worshipped God by giving up her despair, her fear, and her difficult questions. She gave up control and self-sufficiency. She surrendered care of her foster children, her daughter and her husband, even as her eyes were sore with tears. She truly worshipped God by saying along with the psalmists that, "Your love is better than [my and my family's] life" and, in this way, she was confessing, "There is no hope *except in You, Jesus.*" By doing this, she realized that amidst her struggle, God was not "mad at her; He was mad *about her.*" She told us during the last few weeks that she knew now that God never intends for us to suffer. That despite our own fallen nature and susceptibility to sickness and decay, He always wants good for His children. He designed us in His image—perfect, without flaws, and set apart—the definition of Holy. She knew He wanted wholeness and healing for *all* parts of her being.

Amelia helped us learn how to work as one Body, to lift each others' burdens. One particular story that came to life as we met was the story of Moses' people fighting the Amalekites. God told Moses to stand on top of a mountain and to send his people to fight the enemies below. As long as Moses kept his staff raised by holding up his arms, he would be victorious. When he dropped his arms and his staff, he would lose. As this happened and Moses became exhausted and frail, two of his companions let him rest on a rock and *they lifted up his arms and his staff for him.* After admitting she could no longer hold her own arms up to claim victory over this, she allowed us to come in, week after week—by taking her to chemo, by bringing her roses or a meal, by grocery shopping and cleaning her house, by inviting her to swim in our pool and hang out, by crying alongside her—and we held her arms up in victory over the Enemy.

Finally, she showed us that she was indeed perfectly designed by our Creator to be "Amelia." One recurring prayer to God was that He rename Amelia, which means "industrious one," to other names such as "the pearl" or "one who surrenders and rests." We thought she shouldn't have to work so hard all the time. She proved us wrong. During a short period of struggle towards the end, when she described being "in a funk" and tired of fighting, one of the sisters with us told us the story of Jacob wrestling with an angel. Jacob was so determined to be blessed, he wrestled with an angel of God all night long. And he beat the angel. Amelia showed us that she could wrestle with anything—even the power of death—and overcome it with her undaunted commitment to love God, her family, and the lost. When I researched other definitions of Amelia's name, besides "industrious one" I also found "beloved, one who is loved by many" and "One who strives with God." When Jacob beat this angel, the angel blessed him by changing his name to Israel, which also means "One who strives with God."

I am honored to have a God who has positioned me, as part of the women's ministry, to be one small part of this grand and beautifully simple plan. I was put here at this church, in this Body for *one woman*. And Amelia got to usher *me* into the writer Jesus has wanted me to be all these years by trusting me with the most important story. My role in this world has been to be, as inexperienced, as goofy, and as inadequate as I feel, the person who got to see and record raw, sacrificial love expose all the Darkness. I was blessed to have a purpose, to feel as soon as I arrived at Amelia's side to pray with other women for God's perfect will, that *this* is what I am made to do. As another woman who prayed with us told me, this time *I got to be that person* waving my hands in the air frantically, getting anyone and everyone's attention while pointing simultaneously towards Amelia saying passionately, "*There she is. That's Amelia. Right now, she's the one who needs Jesus' love.*" I got to feel what Jesus felt for Amelia when He went to the cross. He died for Amelia, just Amelia, and if she was the only person on earth, He would do it all again. He showed me that Amelia deserved the entirety of His love, and that He could love through us, one person at a time, from "strength to strength," from "glory to glory." By being a part of this singular plan, this forever sisterhood, I have come to believe this is what we're all created for, to know the Father's love through Jesus—together.

Week of Fires, October 2003
Reaching Critical Mass

The San Diego fires had taken over almost all of San Diego. The fires were monomaniacal, traveling down the interstates, jumping over roads and onto peoples' homes, lands, burning virtually everything. Three independent fires consumed everything in their paths from the north, east, and southeast, exhausting every firefighter available in California and neighboring states. By the time the three fires were contained, over 366,000 acres were destroyed, 17 people lost their lives, almost 150 others injured. Even though we live a mile from the ocean, the toxic air outside had us quarantined inside our homes. By order of the mayor and health officials, all windows and doors were to remain closed.

℘

Sitting in, closed in, I got a small break from the events around me. I guess I needed it; in workshop the Wednesday before, I couldn't open my mouth to tell the class that Amelia actually died at 5:22 p.m., the week before the fires began, during our class meeting. I could barely bring myself to walk from work on campus to class. I didn't say anything, even though I wanted to spare the class its useful workshop comments because at that point, I didn't want to think about crafting anything to do with Amelia's story.

Story. That's what it is, but it isn't predictable, a writer can't invent it, and even if it was given to me as a gift from Amelia to share with others, it is certainly not a story I'd want to manipulate at this point in its infancy. I had always wanted a story that would tell itself, using me as a vessel—as hands typing out its existence. I definitely have the story, and I want to be the vessel, I just didn't/couldn't ever imagine it would feel like this. Truly, this is like giving birth—a genuine, wrenching dying to myself so that life might be born.

The first three days home left me with no other resource to distract me from the grieving. That's when it finally collapsed onto me. Either it was the stifled, polluted air, or it was the heaviness of loss pressing its leaden foot into my chest, but it was here.

I woke up every night during the week to do some of the grieving. Usually at 3 a.m., my body could not longer rest, and it woke up to release some of the dross, this *yuck*, inside. I would do a combination of crying, throwing tantrums, breathing shallow, praying and trying to cooperate in mind and spirit to get through this necessary outpouring. Chris would wake up quietly, even though I'd been punching him with unfettered fists and fly-away elbows. He held me as best as he could get his arms around me, or he stroked my head and said it was okay, it was okay, so let it pass out of me. He prayed over me in silence and out loud, and when the fits passed back into deep breathing and the calmness to return me to sleep, he would watch me, sitting over me, until it was over.

One of the last nights of the week, as Chris and I were just going to bed, I felt I was hitting critical mass again, this time just short of midnight.

"It's coming again," I told Chris, and he assured me it was going to be okay. He searched our nightstands but couldn't find our Bible. He got up and went downstairs, lights still off, to look for one. At the moment he left, I was completely terrorized by the darkness. It felt like dozens of pairs of eyes were rushing at me, staring dead at me from all around the room. Every door and window was covered by the influence of these horrible images. I shut my eyes and put my hands over them and began to call out for Chris and Jesus, one or both, whoever could come fastest. My skin, which had been hurting severely from all the bleeding and cracking, couldn't feel anything anymore. I was physically numb, but the level of suffering was still there.

"It's not physical, this attack," I told Chris. He knelt down at the side of the bed and turned immediately to the verse in the Bible. He read out, "For our struggle is not against flesh and blood, but against the rulers, against the authorities, against the powers of this dark world and against the spiritual forces of evil in the heavenly realms." He continued to read from another book about how the light exposes all darkness. He turned on one of the lights. Instantly, I felt in less danger. I turned on the light on my side of the bed.

Then, an image of myself, standing on top of our bed, flashed before me. I refused it as irrational, but it returned. It felt like a picture God was giving me. I didn't want to be foolish; maybe I didn't want to scare Chris, yet I knew somehow I needed to recreate this vision. Instead, I stood up on the floor *next* to the bed, Chris still praying with his head bowed, turning to other verses of encouragement and truth. As I stood praying myself, I heard a very clear, "Don't quench me." I stepped quickly onto the bed and stood in the middle of it, knowing I was supposed to be on top of the bed because even though it was nonsense, God asked me to do it.

Chris looked up at me from his kneeling position, and for lack of explanation, I said—calm and abrupt at the same time, "I'm supposed to do this." He looked just as confused, but he trusted and said, "it's okay," and continued to read and pray.

Then, I saw a picture of me standing with both of my arms raised completely up, head thrown back. Again, I thought I don't want to do this. In the middle of the night, here I was, standing in the middle of our queen bed, lights on, my husband kneeling at my feet, holding my ankles in one hand and praying over an open Bible with the other. It was completely crazy! I didn't want to lift my arms up, so I made a small concession and lifted up just one arm, my right arm, trying to extend my hand up. I thought I could obey in increments. As it happened, I was unable to lift my arm completely up. It fell as soon as I thrust it up, and my hand landed behind my head, my elbow still in the air.

I was a little confused why I couldn't keep my arm up, so I left it where it landed. A few seconds later, eyes still shut, I was back at the hospital bed watching Amelia yank her hand out of her Aunt Amy's, throw it up in the air, and let her hand fall behind her head. It was the same right arm, the same movement, and I realized that this is what I was trying to replicate. The floor was an unacceptable place to stand because it wasn't just about the standing. It was about standing as tall as possible, reaching as high as possible with my arms, and eventually ending up in a position of rest, with my hand relaxed behind my head, just like Amelia.

The clarity was immense. I was trying to stand up, however confused and in pain, and reach out for God. At the hospital, when Aunt Amy was telling Amelia how she was always the "go to" person, the savior of their entire family, Amelia pulled away. It was as if she didn't want that role. She refused to be the person everyone pinned her down to be. She rejected the burden of it all, and in its place she was sitting so straight up she could have been standing. As a final act she was reaching away from her family and Up, and she was freed from everything by this choice. She could relax now because she had her own savior to depend on.

I nodded my head and began to cry. In agreement with what Amelia did, what she was still teaching me even after she had left us, I prayed quietly, "As long as this attack of eczema takes, God, *I still choose you.*" As I released this prayer, I felt like I was given permission to sit back down. I did, and Chris looked up at me. I told him, "I can sit down now," and he got into bed and held me, comforting me that I didn't have to talk about what I was doing or why I thought I was doing it if I wasn't ready to. I asked him to leave all the lights on until I fell asleep.

☙

We called Dane to invite him and Emily over, spend time with us and our other friends who had evacuated and came to stay with us at our place in OB. He said he would spend time with Kristine and her family so Emily could play with her four daughters, and that he was doing "unusually well." I guess the distraction of the fires—of someone else's tragedy—although it rendered us San Diegans helpless to fight for our land and homes because we had been ordered not to do anything but donate to the Red Cross, gave Dane a hidden blessing of not thinking about his own loss.

Dane asked Chris the week before, when Chris dropped off dinner for them, if he could call me at home because he wanted to know what he described as, "what Ella's spirit sensed" during the last hours of Amelia's life. He mentioned wanting to get confirmation on some things that he, himself, was feeling about what Amelia was going through and trying to communicate without words. Chris reminded me of this and said maybe because the week was slow, I could go over there and spend some time talking with Dane.

By the week of the fires, every single person I know called to offer support in practical ways—bring food to Dane and Emily, clean their house, give money. And always, always there was the footnote, "we're praying for them and for you especially, Ella, because we know how much you gave to Amelia." I still felt guilty. *I don't deserve this much attention. I'm embarrassed, I'm not the one who needs this support,* I kept thinking. I heard them ask me on the machine to call them back so they could help; I read similar e-mails from all the other friends. I watched my skin crack and bleed horrifically because of the utterly polluted air I was breathing. I slathered on lotion, ointment, and medication on my face, neck, and shoulders. I cried in fear because I didn't think I had anything left in me that could fight this onslaught of sickness if it was coming back again, but I also knew I wasn't going to be alone in the struggle, and that if I could just make the same choice each time I felt the quickening of depression, it was all I needed to do.

And yet, although the small epiphany that night on my bed gave me something to go back to, and even though people were calling, writing, and coming up to me at church to pray for me, at home, I was becoming too choked up with those last memories, with emotions, with the expectancy of every Known and Unknown side of grief and sickness to call anyone back who could come over and help keep this weight from getting heavier.

Months later, I still haven't returned the calls or e-mails.

High Achievements and Honors

Falling Off, One More

We fall off our wagons.
One more drink
One more smoke

One more hour at work
instead of at home
at the "for now" job going on five years

One more hour at the bar
at the racetrack
at the mall
at his whim
under her abuse
stuck in their tradition their ways not mine

One more compromise

Where when why how you do it and somehow
somewhere someday you're not feeling the home,
it's gone, you've moved out,
left your ideas that one great idea that broke off
of the larger dream and now
weighs empty in the back seat of your car,
or life

Moving, sad and afraid in OB for so many
on the move, "camping" they say,
who have become fixtures, beachside furniture,
on this sandbox [sandboxed in]
some living room huh

Found myself praying
for their lives to feel peaceful for, after all,
clothes don't make a man and the same clothes
so weathered, even tough—it looks like armor—don't
protect the gentle person inside, so maybe
just maybe this person is full of the soft sides of joy and love
(what are those words anymore)
who am I to judge or presume tattered outside means
falling apart inside, too.

Though somehow I know it's not all true,
that the joy they find in their day might be
a morsel of—no not food that's not all they're hungry for—
but a scrap of hope
from a conversation with another transient
or a smooth jam session
with the guy who tends his guitar precious to him
like the other's dog, man's best friend.

Or maybe the warmth of a borrowed piece of bonfire,
everyone sitting low buzzing high

The search persists for the one lost sheep
out of the hundreds
more like thousands
did you know every night in America
six to seven hundred thousand people go homeless,
a third of them kids
            all of them orphans,
what I had the knot for in the pit of my ignorance
was for our one friend our good friend Marty
who didn't come home one night and then
two weeks later we hear he's off the wagon again

we fall off our wagons.
One more drink
One more smoke

One more hour at work
instead of at home
at the "for now" job going on sixteen years

One more hour at the bar
at the racetrack
at the mall
at his whim
under her abuse
stuck in their tradition their ways not mine

One more hour pretending we don't see that
accepting the un-acceptable
wearing our badge of denial
One more compromise

Apparently it happens harder during the holidays
or simply because holidays remind us
the days can be hollow
and the black hole pulls nonspecific nondescript
little things we let go by
because why do we care,
but this is our friend Marty, these are his little things
disappeared: first his pen, then his spiralled notes,
his no braces smile,
then his gel-tempered curls, his grass stain
green jeans, his corner of the constellations
and his right to the throne of life

We didn't care so much for the daily six hundred thousand
we only used our eyes to turn over faces and guitars
and hunched over bundles of suspect-joy on the beach
for our one friend our good friend our
lost friend. If we had to, interrogate each grain of sand,
ask who's seen him on the beach wall or up Newport
looking for cheap Chinese food
or anything hearty
because where his heart is these days
even *he* can't feel through the Numb.

Through this lens of the one we've lost,
the one we call by name, sudden concern
for all of them boils me,
the thought of how much they have to carry
on their backs. I understand that's why

they can't stay anywhere, own anything,
have any other responsibilities.
No free hands to do all those things,
to lift anything new up with the old hooks,
the rusty anchors to drag around.
And I know without asking,
most of the time it is not their fault.
We push ourselves away, turn our startled eyes
from the ones who ask. When we deny them
we deny more than spare change,
we refuse them the chance to talk,
be recognized, tell us their names,

can we spare *this* change?

Instead we rename them Invisible, Annoying, Uncomfortable
forget the more clever titles:

transient
veteran
on the outside
camper
ephemeral
temporarily homeless
disenfranchised
shadows
not somebody anymore, just *some body*

In a turn, I revolve back to our one friend who needs,
and maybe we can help him lift the hooks out
throw the anchors into the ocean for passing ships
who might need spare weight.
All I know is, he's not a ship,
not a barge to load things on and let sail.
He's one part of the Greater who needs
the freedom (what does that mean again?)

we fall off our wagons.
One more drink
One more smoke

One more hour at work
at the "for now" job going on five sixteen seventy years

One more hour at the bar
at the racetrack
at the mall
at his whim
under her abuse
stuck in their tradition their ways not mine

One more hour not dealing
ignoring the knot in the pit of
finding distractions call them entertainment
say next time I'll go straight home
next time I'll *just say no*
next time I'll ask for help
next time but this time

Just one more.

What if what if
the next time we fall, we break open
dig in, even help ourselves
tear apart
achieve bottom.
Because when we hit bottom,
who cares who is worse off than we are?
Our bottom means there's no place lower
for me for you for him.

DARE to go straight home,
to fall on our face, admit weakness,
say we can't do it on our own.
DARE to only look up, extend our hands,
to feel, leak, explode out, to need.
DARE to breathe in what's waiting,
risk desperation being broken yields freedom.
DARE to surrender.

What happens then?

Going for Gold

Am I the last to discover Natalie Coughlin, Olympic swimmer, was born in my hometown, went to my alma mater (Go Bears), and is part Filipino? Bet she's my "little" cousin! I'm telling folks I taught her everything she knows: which Vallejo thrift store has the best retrofunk clothes, what food stand has the filling-est nutella crepes to lipsmack during study breaks in Berkeley, and the healthiest ground turkey lumpia recipe for family potlucks (one *must* stay fit for Olympic training). What's homegirl teaching me? Truly, if local Pinay Bear can go for Gold, then anything's possible for me, too.

Touched a gold medal once. The volleyball Olympian was at a beachside bar after Athens, buzzing off free drinks, the closest I've come to that level of spectacular self-discipline and accomplishment. My husband's employee gave him her One Year sober coin, thankful for requiring she join AA in exchange for her job, home, life. Makes me think of toll collectors who touch coins everyday, some from people who have crossed oceans, pouring themselves out to secure their children's livelihoods. True Champions are everywhere, never dropping a shift, an eyelid, a breath.

We're closer to glory more often than we know.

Facebook Status:
Ella's eczema is no longer a threat.
Finally.

Facebook is like a regular e-mail account but with extra extras. It's like thinking you're going to go get coffee with an old friend from college at 7-11 and sit outside in your ten year-old Toyota pick-up truck to catch up after losing touch fifteen years ago. But you walk past the façade of 7-11 and get ushered to sit down at a white clothed table for two. Tiered gourmet petit fours and canapés await you, and you get handed a menu of luxurious teas and exotic coffees. You're at high tea, and you take your time sipping loose leaf, steeped goodness while you take a bite of your pumpkin scone dusted with Madagascar vanilla, having that heart-to-heart conversation.

Or, if the high tea metaphor doesn't fascinate you, Facebook is like e-mail on steroids. Besides the visual explosion on Facebook—with a picture linked to each person's name, you can create photo albums of your life, update your profile with what you do, where you've been—there are unlimited goofy interactions you can dive into, like playing Scrabble with your fourth grade classmate, sending San Miguel beer or *pancit palabok* to other Filipinos (or Asianfiles who ate the noodles at friends' houses), posting current news articles, or uploading MTV's first "America's Best Dance Crew" champs, Jabbawockeez, YouTube dance clips. You can even write a "note"* where you describe your trip to India in

---

* I'm instructed that "Notes" on Facebook are basically the same as blogposts except you don't have to wrestle with the idea of having an entire blog all for your own thoughts (and maybe, you avoid possible ego-inflation and/or the risk of losing the ability to verbally communicate with non-cyber-mediated humans).

a narrative poem, or you can try to explain your political process in a post called "Why I'm Still Voting for Obama (aka, GASP! The Abortion Talk!)." You can virtually catch up with high school classmates by skimming over their posts, Profile and Photo pages before you connect about what's happening now (*if* you have lingering questions, that is).

One of the best features is that this is an optional social network; you choose to join it and become "friends" with people who are also part of it. A highlight of my day is seeing that certain people I've known throughout my life have "found me" or I've found them here, and we've asked to be "friends" again. I have reconnected with my BFF (Best Friend Fred) from high school and college, my double dutch partner from grade school, my cousins after we mutually fell away post-parental divorce, former instructors, former students, my half-brother in the Philippines, and everyone in between.

If you join and don't get mildly addicted like I have, the quick version of seeing how friends are doing are these one-liners next to each person's name. They're called "Status Updates," and if people want, they can type quick narratives of how they're doing at that moment. "Steve Linke is going to Guys' Night Out—bowling, beer, and bros." "Samer Farhat just had the best bike ride this morning." "Michelle Brown Rivero is watching Cal kick some Stanfurd butt!" "Patricia Mendoza is disheartened at the tragedy in Mumbai." "Chris Baron is not lost."

I reconnected with one of my best girlfriends from our freshman dorm in Berkeley. After our euphoric woo-hoos and looking at each others' photo albums (I posted ones for our son and daughter from their births to their recent birthday picnic, she posted playing bass in the NYC band she's in and snaps from her trip to Ireland), we started backtracking to fill each other in on the last ten years or so. Eventually, we were overwhelmed with the pressure to share, so we decided to serve each other tidbits, about five at a time, inspired by the ad on a package of grape tomatoes: "five a day."

The handful of grape tomatoes below eventually came after my former classmate asked how my eczema was doing. She remembered my small patches in undergrad and has had to pursue significant diet and lifestyle changes herself because eczema also had been plaguing her body. It's an excerpt from our Facebook exchanges.

Onto some eczemic 411:

*First eruption in 1997, moved to Hawai'i. I began getting the full body allergy testing every six months to a year at this point. My diet drastically changed b/c I was allergic to SO many foods like chicken, beef, lentils, walnuts, basically everything besides rice and corn (not allergic to yeast though...boo for you).

My body healed after that.

*Second eruption began in 2000. After we got married and the acupuncture/holistic tea stuff petered out, Chris started watching me sink. I shudder thinking how painful the eczema was on our wedding day. Chris couldn't even touch me. I actually saved myself for him (ahem, after throwing myself at a buncha guys through the years before meeting him!). We couldn't actually touch each other for about *two years* after we married b/c my skin was oozing, bleeding, peeling, and I could never sleep from the insomnia. I had to get on psych. meds for depression, then insomnia, and was close to getting on them for panic/ anxiety disorder until my cousins and mom sent me to a residential rehab place for 3 weeks just three months after we married (Oct. 2001, a month after 9/11).

*The place basically changed my life. We went vegan for 3+ years and loved it. No guilt, and lots of regular poops in between tofu meals! I also had to walk 5 miles a day while learning how to reset my thinking (an Old Testament prayer type of walk where you start with thankfulness for everything you have, then reminding yourself who God is, then praying for others, then finally, after some confessing of distractions within yourself, you "enter" a quiet place of being, just Being with God and sharing your needs, etc.)

*During the rehab place, my depression broke. Insomnia didn't leave for another year and a half. I can't express how much I will never take sleeping for granted! No more panic attacks either. And all the walking made my butt less big and squishy (I gained lots of weight trying crazy ass diets (big crazy ass!) suggested by the acupuncturists--t he most famous one: add two tablespoons of this oil called Udos to each meal. It was like 800 more calories a day! She said it would lube my internal organs and spread out to my skin. Biotch. She was skinny, too, but she ate it everyday herself. I think she had a cracked brain she was trying to lube.

*Anywho: along with all the physical rehab I was trying and the diet/lifestyle change, I started being recommended by my pastors to go to any/all healing services/trainings I could go to. It worked out b/c I had to quit the grad program and working in order to heal for 9 months. So, I went. And I learned that what I learned from my mom's faith and what I interpreted on my own about sickness and healing were totally erroneous and very contrary to what Jesus taught about. I thought I knew enough! I went to teachings, small meetings, big meetings, got a mentor who loves to teach others about healing prayer, and I got my mind straight on what I thought I believed.

*There were years of prayers that happened with people in my community (and strangers in different churches too), but I would say the one turning point prayer for me was at my mentor's home. She had a monthly Women's Bible Study at her house for 14 years, and I heard about it (she wasn't my mentor yet). A woman I was friends with who had end stage breast cancer (sadly, she died four years ago) told me she was going to check it out and I should come along. Totally desperate for any light, I went. Went around the room introducing ourselves (about 15 women from 19-75 yrs old, every color, from SD, some from Orange County, all different churches). My cheesy intro included something like, "I guess I'm here b/c I want to learn how to live with my disease and still love and serve God." There was a woman across from me on the couch, and she shot up and bolted to my side. She said, "Ella, I had MS for ten years, but we are not created to suffer like this. It is NOT God's plan for anyone to be sick. He healed me completely, and He wants to do that for you, too. It is NOT his plan for you to *"learn how to live with a disease!"* We can ask for healing from this!"

Forty-five minutes later, I am on the floor sweating, hair out of its hair tie, women holding me up b/c I was basically bawling, screaming, shaking, everything. The Christianese term when one passes out is "slain in the Spirit." But, since I was on the floor looking possessed, a funny Christianese term is "shakin' and bakin." Pretty apropos. I didn't hear anything they prayed (I heard one Mexican woman praying in Spanish among many other indiscernible, "prayer tongues" while I was in and out of it), but when I opened my eyes, the "smoke" cleared. I felt 100% peace. Could not will not try to explain it. (Incidentally, while I keeled over and was flopping around, my friend with cancer also fell over b/c someone got a vision of leeches on someone's vertebrae, and she came there ready to tell them they found more cancer on her vertebrae...so apparently the prayer meeting was also very efficient, as I've learned God happens to be with teaching me things!)

Okay, so there's a story in the Hebrew text (Old Testament) about this wise guy named Gideon who is asked to do something for God. He's strong in faith, but he just needs some reassurance. So, he tells God, "Okay, I'll do it, but FIRST, you gotta show me you did tell me to do this thing. I'm going to put out my fleece blanket (a real animal hide back then, not Old Navy), and in the morning, when the grass has dew on it from the night, my fleece better be dry." Paraphrasing. When Christians suggest we should ask for confirmation for something we think is from God, they say, "You should check the fleece." (Gideon's fleece was dry in the wet grass, so allegedly he should've continued on his mission. Ha! He still chickened out and asked for another test...ah, how human we are).

*I went home and told Chris I felt healed. But, I happened to have my yearly allergy test the next morning. I said to him, "I'm no stupid (or faithful enough!) chick. I could skip the test b/c I feel so good about the prayer, BUT you KNOW I'm going to check the fleece!" More paraphrase.

Testing day, all the dozens of little shots, all the itching but having to sit still (Chris held me down). The allergist read my results and said, "Basically, your results are amazingly unamazing. You are allergic to Nothing."

That was it for the allergies. I didn't have the guts to switch back from vegan to eating normal right away (what was normal before that anywho? I was always restricted from something here and there). That didn't come until I got prego in 2005 and couldn't stand the sight of veggies. I wanted KFC and Taco Hell! (Actually, on our first and only trip to Europe in '04, I dreamt of getting to eat the food, so I just went for it and returned to vegan when we got back.)

My inside was healed, but the outside took another two years to clear up. But, I totally knew the darkest part of the night was over. My whole attitude was resurrected. The pain was going to retreat, and I was going to see the rest of my body heal. I had to keep walking away, in faith, from my personal Egypt--that place of bondage--and keep reminding myself the desert I'd been in *did* provide for me, even if it seemed like simple necessities (manna, the company of my family and friends, and sometimes, a cloud by day to follow).

How 'bout them grape tomatoes?

Routine Worship

September 11, 2005

Sunday worship in the school auditorium,
in back—my usual place—I could stand
without claustrophobic seats ganging up on me.
People trickling, handling krispy kremes, caffeine,
bulletins. Some, Bibles. Singing, trying to "get"
to "that holy place," I saw the foster child laboring,
rolling his walker. Kinky hair, latte-colored
chubby cheeks, loose-jaw smile were framed
by shrugged shoulders as twisted arms knotted
around metal handles. They carried
his withered legs, heavy sneakers dragging behind
—obviously for fashion, not function.
I prayed, "Lord, heal," obligatory, as I lamented,
It isn't fair, is it? Faithless—unsure,
still trying to get to "that" place.

November 6, 2006

Routine worship. I spotted the disabled boy
walker scratch-rolling, one-sided leaning.
Suddenly, a blink. Clarity sharpened.
Heaven began swirling terrestrial.
Soon, every person coming in: visibly
maimed. Crutches, wheelchairs, canes.
Wracked, malformed, amputated.
Gaping, desperate, nowhere to conceal
brokenness. I began to shake, crying and nodding
my head in assent. I knew He was answering
nagging questions of unfairness. He knew

if I saw how fragmented we are—all needing palettes
lowered by our friends at Jesus' feet—if I saw everyone's
insides on the outside, too,
I could see through his lens,
sense compassion,
his resolve towards wholeness.

Souplantation

Souplantation: dream escape. It recalls once-vegan diet, finding more than two things to eat when dining. Verdant, rainbowed salads usher regularity... Now omnivorous, clam chowder, cheesied foccacia and chocolate lava cake are savored. Souplantation safeguards leisurely luxuries of picking and choosing what to plate and bowl. Beyond my routine of eating toddler leftovers—two-bite-swallow-gulp-water-drive-mini-van—I exploit multiple eating muscles at the Plantation. *Slurp, crunch, chew, sip, lick, roll, suck, grind.* This culinary orgy creates the illusion I have time, time, time. None seated in surrounding tables suspect my indulgence, probably because they're salivating in their own liberating fantasies. *Roll. Suck. Grind.*

Reason, Season, Life

If every person we meet is for "reason, season or life," how do I move him from reason (student needing class) and season (we now eat Thai occasionally) to life (I wanna know how his partner died, what authors his humility, why does he believe in our friendship)? Of what I can possibly offer him (open heart and ears, longing to pray him Up, resolution to repent for categorical, Christian discrimination), trying to be part of any answer for him—as we all seek—may mean glaring at my reflection, maybe discovering an ugly, confused hypocrite, mournfully unversed in loving.

Washed and Worn

with Chris Baron

It was the height (more aptly, depth) of insomnia. I lay in bed, trying to cry and scratch noiselessly so as not to wake Chris, trying to will myself to float above the bed because the sheets were already stained with Aquaphor ointment, prescription lotion, blood, skin cells, and weeping from fissured skin, corners of eyes. I was on the third medication supposedly to address the insomnia, a secondary problem set off by the year-long eczema flare-up, yet I couldn't get to sleep before 6 or 7 a.m. each day. By that point, I was wiped out from the battle with myself during the night, so sleep finally won. If I didn't have to wake up an hour later to go teach my class at SD State, I slept obliviously until 1 or 2 in the afternoon, woke in a hazy dread, anticipating the torturous day and night ahead.

I am not an organized man. But I can say that I like order, and with each passing day the chaotic whirlwind of my engagement-wedding-honeymoon-and now re-entry was diffusing into some routine. Along with this transi-

tion came the desire for some kind of structure to be restored. It began at home. Waking up early with the sun filtering in through the old blinds of our bedroom window, I found Ella, finally, snoring, her eyes closed, her breathing a beautiful and contorted melody. I fell asleep with prayers on my lips for just such a song, and I hoped as I quietly put my feet on the floor that she had been like this since before the sun came up.

For months, Chris had been taking me to a few Ross stores to buy larger, all-cotton clothes—doctors' orders—to try and let my tormented skin breathe. As soon as I put a new piece on, it was sticky with ointment and flecked with my sheddings. Each day, the new clothes ended up in the office/guest room of our apartment, looking instantly old and decayed. With each cadavered clothing, I became a more disabled participant in the housekeeping. I couldn't wash dishes because my fingers were like the rest of my body, alternating between itchy and painful but always cracked and bleeding. I had no appetite for food so didn't cook. I couldn't go to the Laundromat across the street because that meant addressing the laundry and seeing my disease in disarrayed states, one t-shirt or loose workout pants at a time.

I wandered into the office to turn the computer on and start the morning by checking e-mail.

It was left on, and Ella had been writing the night before, into the early morning, some story for an anthology on interracial marriage. The keys were still glossy with Aquaphor and tubes of lotion piled against the screen. What got me most were the Kleenex wadded and thrown all over, having absorbed her depressive fits, and then of course, the flakes of skin that Ella missed even in her rabid spurts of cleaning. They were part of us; her skin, scratched to pieces, everywhere.

Our pile was impossible. In commiserating with me, Chris didn't lead by example and do his laundry all those months, either. The only clothes he did get cleaned were his "teacher button ups," but he dropped those off at the dry cleaners and picked them up after work.

But it wasn't the littered ashes of skin, or the stacks of paper pooling on the desk, and it wasn't the not-yet-paid bills, or the essays that needed to be graded. It was the piles and piles of clothes that grew in heaps along our closet floors and now flooded out into the common area, clothes piled in chairs full of dirt and skin, unattended and left in tiredness and apathy.

When we couldn't open the door to the second room, Chris came up with an idea.

It was time I thought, today, to clean the shit out of these clothes.

I was excited because I had a project, and in the youth of my marriage I saw this as a way of serving our family, of maybe making Ella happy even for a minute. Her joy was so fleeting now, and it seemed preposterous to even try to make her laugh. The notion of giving her this tangible gift gave me wings. I began piling the laundry by the door, then organizing it into giant trash bags. The more I piled the clothes—months and months worth of clothes—and pushed them into trash bags, the plastic bulging and ripping until I double bagged them, I found myself face to face with what seemed like an insurmountable task. Literally.

In the midst of my stuffing, I heard the quiet groans of Ella waking. The unsaid rule was "undisturbance" of the sleeping and aching wife. Usually, when she finally would stir, I would become filled up with childlike expectation and rapt delight of a newlywed. But often, and even now, the truth was swollen, hands squeezing, eyes tightly shut, her mouth still soft, whispering quietly.

I bent down close, and I began to excitedly, as if to distract her, tell her about my plan for the laundry. Often, in these moments of newly-hatched plans, I had initial expectations of approval, but soon, I'd find myself swimming in doubt. Did she want me to do it? Then, some frustration. Couldn't she see that this was good for us? I calmly and quietly explained

*how I would always do this kind of thing, fluff
and fold, for my own laundry when it began
to pile up. I promised the joy of dirty bags of
clothes returned anew in papered packages soft
and tightly folded.*

He told me, "I know what to do. I'll put
all of our laundry in a shopping cart from
the Appletree grocery store and bring our
clothes to the Laundromat next to it. The
sign says it's only 99 cents a pound to wash,
dry, and fold."

Thoroughly dumbed down by the insomniac hours of the night before, I was trying
to listen to Chris' proposal while on the
verge of passing out. Plus, being the inher-
ently cheap Asian that I was, I was hesitant.

But Chris came back with, "I used to do
fluff and fold all the time when I lived in
Hillcrest. It's a great deal, and they're done
the same day."

I shrugged, agreed we should do it
because I wasn't going to, and buying more
misfit clothes at Ross for my ill-fitting skin
seemed the worse economic crime.

*She looked at me, puzzled either about my
strange enthusiasm for such a thing, or maybe
because, as new roommates, we were still discovering one another's morning mannerisms.
And that was one of countless new ways of
living we were trying our hands at, such as
how an Upper East Side Manhattan-bred,
blond-haired, green-eyed Jewish man could*

find common ground with a middle class, sub-urban child of Filipino immigrants—brown skin, almond eyes, English as a second language, and all. Nonetheless, I was determined to get this one thing done.

I wasn't there when he took the clothes. I mean, I was in the apartment, but I wasn't "there" there. He shared his project with me sometime mid-morning-lark-serenade, right when a bird was humming, *R.E.M., R.E.Mmmmm.* Somehow, I sleep-grog-walked from the bedroom to our now-emptied office. That room faced the sun, and I wanted some light through the undraped window.

When I left her lying there in her blanketed cocoon, I remembered something else.

On our honeymoon, in the midst of my elation in running through the airport to make our connecting flight, I ran straight to a flight attendant passing by and asked if the gate was just ahead. She smiled and pointed, and as I ran, I could see Ella slowing her pace. She was staring at me with a look I had seen before, but not from her. It was a sense of utter disappointment: not in me, but circling around me, as if she was looking at something that had come and left again. I walked back to her and took her hand.

"C'mon. Why did you do that?" she looked at me.

Her eyes swollen a bit, tired now. I could only look at her. She pointed to signs all around and to screens filled with red numbers and words confirming where we were supposed to go. I understood.

"But they work here," I said. "What's wrong with asking them?"

She started to shuffle along. It is difficult for someone who hasn't experienced this type of severe eczema to understand the complexity of simple motions. Every action is tripled in its efforts, and every movement causes the body to react into itself with pain and desperate response. This walking was wearisome enough, but the frustration caused by what Ella called later, Entitlement, was even more taxing for her. The newness of marriage was intense; with its newness came the exhaustion of learning to love and serve. And with the illness came the disappointing revelation of **not** *loving and* **not** *serving.*

I wondered if somehow my fluff-and-fold adventure was spinning around my bed as entitlement, as another way that Chris, because he's a "white man," gets what he wants when he wants because he always has, after all. She didn't disagree, so I quieted the voices when I could, and I began to find my way back to the garbage bags.

I crossed Santa Monica Boulevard, nabbed a red shopping cart from the Appletree market, piled five trash bags filled with clothes into the top and bottom, and wheeled my way to the ocean Laundromat. I dropped the clothes at the counter, smiling at the woman, her stare unflinching as she sorted them into even more detailed piles. The sign behind her read, "Fluff and Fold, 99cents/lb." Still smiling, I folded the garbage bags under my arm.

I went back to check on Ella, but she was fast asleep, so I grabbed my shoes and headed to the OB Rec to play some hoops while the laundry continued its own journey.

On my walk, I considered all the ways that this might be different. The relief of making such a tangible contribution to our family washed over me for a moment. Perhaps a little bit of organization was all we needed. Maybe the stress and chaos were damaging Ella's immune system, exacerbating it.

I thought about the whole issue of entitlement, too. Would it be better if I had washed all the clothes myself? This led me down a whole rabbit trail of untruths and ideas that made me want to fully unpeel any entitlement by working my ass off. Maybe it was because I was so tired, or maybe it was because I had imagined getting Ella to come help me but remembered that she would/could not. Maybe it was because I couldn't help thinking about how much I wished that she would just be better, and that I could be an unbridled newlywed.

I was angry. The anger led me down other thought trails; I imagined the lecture I might get about once again living an entitled life. For her, maybe the packages of laundry would just be further evidence of some kind of grand mis-

*take we had made in getting married. Maybe
our cultures were just too different and that
these acts meant to be loving only revealed
sharp differences of values that could never be
reshaped.*

*She is an Asian woman from a huge com-
munity struggling to find herself among the
crowd. And I am a Jewish kid inflicted with
a long history and heritage of scrapping and
struggling to just survive. As Jews, sometimes
the only way to survive, to be heard, to press
on, is to claim entitlement, to stand against
being perpetually displaced from land, from
family, from resources. Jews used entitlement
as a voice, and especially now, as an antidote
for the poisons of the past. Never Again.*

*I stood there for a time, remembering
myself.*

*I took any frustrations that I had about my
newlywed life on the basketball court. It could
be said by some that these were the days of my
best hoops. I left every ounce of agony, every
image of Ella's scratching fingers, every fleck of
dry skin, every frustrated moment of my new
wife sleeping away the day, every downcast and
shaming stare, every self-defeating word that
made me feel useless. All were washed away
in the sweat and pounding of that old gym,
and when I walked out of that dark place, I
could remember her like sunlight. I could see
her unbloodied and unworn skin, and on this
particular day, I saw that the chaos was real,
but it was a chaos in her mind, a craziness that
was consuming her, and that no matter how*

much laundry we ever did, it was her mind
that needed to be washed clean.

Still, it wasn't going to hurt that the laun-
dry would be utterly clean and folded.

It was a thing of beauty when I arrived.
Christmas morning at the OB Wash, my blue
packages wrapped tightly with industrial
string.

In between states of wakefulness, exhaustion, delirium, and confusion, I heard a constant squeaking outside. Not unlike Ocean
Beach's mixed bag of renters and transients,
I had heard stranger noises, including the
gang of wild parrots squawking aggressively
in overhead palm trees. Soon, I realized the
squeaking was a shopping cart, and it was
coming in the direction of our apartment.
After a pause, I heard Chris open the door.
He came in with two packages wrapped
in blue paper. It reminded me of the pink
butcher paper Sam used to wrap the meat in
for his favorite customer, Alice, on her way
home to roast a loin (and maybe ice Mar-
cia's swollen nose or do speech therapy with
Cindy in between), of the way the two once-
tragically-broken families somehow re-inte-
grated and lived the exceptionally "typical"
suburban Brady Bunch life. Maybe if we
had an Alice, we'd be reconciled with this illness and generally okay ourselves, planning
trips to the Grand Canyon and Honolulu,
having only to be wary of getting lost (in
both places!) and taboo tikis instead of how

to do our laundry and preserve our façade of
being afloat despite the daily sinking.

*I filled the cart with one after another, and
still they kept coming. Package after package
until the cart was overflowing, arms aching
a bit. An exorbitant amount rang onto the
metallic cash register, and the woman didn't
even look up.*

*"One hundred fifty pounds of laundry?
Give or take." She quietly said.*

*She ran my credit card, and I stood there in
shock for a moment then began the trek back
to our apartment. I remember the bumpiness
of the parking lot, the shrill squeaking of shopping cart wheels spinning out of control.*

*I parked the cart at the base of the stairs,
and I bravely walked up, two of the bundles
footballed under my arms. Ella was asleep and
awake on our blue futon in the office, and I
wandered in and set the packages down near
her feet. I gently kissed her forehead.*

*"Ella," I said quietly, "I have to tell you
something."*

She unsquinted her eyes and half-smiled.

I was lying on his college futon, the navy
blue cover now also needing a scrub as my
skin rubbed against it. Chris came over to
the room, put the two packages down, and
knelt by my face, a guilty smile on his face.

"Ella," he said quietly, "I have to tell you
something."

I couldn't sit up to be responsive; a clear memory of these early afternoon wake-ups is that it felt like someone had their steel-toed army boot on my face and neck. Until Chris lifted me up or I lay there for more hours, I literally could not move my head from wherever it lay. I looked at him from my pinned position, tried to smile, and he leaned in.

"I went to pick up our laundry and pay for it." He looked around and hushed his voice. "Ella, the laundry is done, but we had a hundred and fifty pounds of it."

> *"Ella, the laundry is done, but…we had one hundred fifty pounds of it."*

I didn't react yet, couldn't, so Chris motioned for me to wait and left the room. He retrieved the rest of our blue butcher-papered laundry—8 or 10 bags, each the size of an 80s breakdancing boom box. The floor was re-carpeted with these sky blue bags of laundry, and both of us took in the new upholstery.

> *I waited for her reaction, but there wasn't one. She wasn't being cold, only silent. I motioned for her to wait, and I made trip after trip with package after package until they covered the floor like a tiny blue city of skyscrapers.*

We didn't say anything for several minutes. I felt a grand mix of shame and awe at how extravagantly stupid we were to pay the 150 dollars for laundry that would have cost us a tenth of that to do ourselves.

At the start of our honeymoon, we had our first married argument at the Tahiti airport. It was a month after 9-11, and Chris' trendy goatee got him and his bags searched at the start, middle, and end of every boarding and deplaning line. By association, every stitch of me and my belongings got searched each time as well. (Never mind that he looked All-American with his 6'4" athletic build, blond-streaked, pomade-spiked hair in his long sleeve surf tee and flip flops, and I could not look less threatening in my stereotypically petite Asian body, a well-worn Roxy, beach hoodie framing lazy, ponytailed long, unbrushed hair. I might've passed as an islander, like a local Tahitian dancer in between luau side jobs.)

We were late to catch our connecting flight. I began reading the walls for arrows, signs in English, French, any language that I could follow. Chris walked immediately up to every person in some sort of uniform—without discerning/asking if any of them actually worked at the airport—and boldly, expectantly asked where we should go to get to our destination. Could've been my habit of being an invisible Asian woman was already challenged by being callously profiled with my "bearded" husband as a conspicuous terrorist, so by this point, I was desperate to get back to being unnoticed by anyone/everyone.

The last thing I wanted us to do was to point ourselves out as targets, then as people who were not resourceful. This was not a Filipino thing to do—depend on strangers, those who were not family, to ask for help much less expect help. I was infuriated by our lack of independence and ability, of my lack as a "good" Asian, to follow directions and rules already set out for us at the airport. I mean, what were those arrows and signs made for? Not decoration.

I felt my shame, his arrogance. Then the word was skywritten over the first day in Tahiti: Entitled. I was so incensed; I could not explain my outrage to Chris. He was confused and so taken by surprise at my disgust of him asking for directions that he had to wait for me to calm down to ask why I was red-faced, teary-eyed, and already wondering if our marriage was a mistake.

Maybe it was because we were committing a crime, literally, by marrying our laundry. Basic logic says you never mix whites with even one drop of color.

And now, not long after that incident, here we were again, looming giants in bundles of clothes cleaned by hands we didn't know, entitlement scoffing back at me. However, this time, I also felt extravagantly loved by Chris, that he would even dare to do this for us—newlyweds in a beachside apartment, me without a job or foreseeable future degree or career to help pay our bills, he working the same job as before we married, now with wedding debt of thousands on his credit cards, having to support an incompetent wife while trying to preserve any semblance of a composed home life, clean laundry one part of it.

Interestingly, in their own unselfconscious and selfless ways, when all of our friends and family helped us, they never made me feel I was acting entitled. Maybe it was because our friends were so gentle with us: bringing us meals, praying for us, visiting me even though I couldn't bear to leave the apartment as the insomnia wrangled my brain chemicals to start seizing my body with panic attacks.

True, we had no other choice but to live in the light with this disease, so much of our pain the spotlight of our community. But, if I'm honest, in an ironic way, what made this taking and *not* giving comfortable was that it was familiar. It felt like pity. Even though being pitied is something No One—regardless of color, age, or religion—wants to be, I could connect with it because I was a master at pity. I pitied myself at every turn, and if these people weren't daily reminders that I didn't have to live like this, especially because our faith was about restoration and preserved dignity in the midst of it, I would have made a religion out of Pity. Nevertheless, because everyone poured into us freely, we simply drank without protest. We made a decision **not** to hide the pain we were in, mostly because we didn't know how else to dilute it, and since Jesus told us walking in "fellowship with each other" like this led to Life, there was no better time to take this step of faith.

Still, all this taking from others was, at its worst, pity, and at its best, the thing I feared. In asking for what I needed, or in letting Chris ask for me, I was acting entitled. But this felt *good*, even healing. The air clearing, I could see and finally empathize with what Chris grew up falling back on and pushing forward with.

When circumstances became extreme, I was raised to keep working—harder—but not to say a word, so no one would notice the problems, and they would eventually be addressed by the right people. In inclement weather, don't rock the boat even more; don't wake the sleeping captain and ask how to navigate the storm. Let the others who should know better fix what's wrong. *Don't make things worse by interfering. Stand aside. Be invisible.* For Chris, he was raised to understand extreme conditions, if left alone, could end catastrophically. He was taught to do the opposite: wake up the captain, gather forces, ask for more resources, and do what needs to be done to make it through the storm. *Don't make things worse by standing still. Be assertive. Do something.*

Maybe, for some, acting "entitled" in certain situations, like having to compensate for centuries of anti-Semitism, like trying to endure rootlessness from forced diasporas, like immigrating from the Philippines under a promise of being called and regarded legitimate Americans, like being chronically sick and needing tons of help even though it was counterintuitive to emerge from the shadows, is not only okay, it's the right and moral thing to do.

Could it be possible that this journey might show me how to move from being the *Un*titled to being the *En*titled because I'm not a second class citizen, never had to be, and I do deserve fundamental rights, including abundant support, health, and confidence? Could it be that a truth of our new life together as husband and wife—blending white and color to make new, varied, finer shades on the spectrum—was beginning to make itself at home, right there next to resurrected and restructured cotton towers?

We confessed how we felt to each other. And then, we promised not to tell anyone just yet about this indiscretion. Maybe we wanted to hold onto this one thing, this secret if you will, because it was the only piece of us that everyone else didn't have to know or deal with. Because even as the revelation was new blood in the veins, if everyone knew absolutely everything about us trying to deal with this excruciating existence we were in the middle of, we might have to face even more reality than we could possibly bear, good *and* bad. Under the weight we were already trying to shoulder—with everyone's help—adding an ounce of this new, ridiculous way that we tried to cope would definitely break the camel's back, much less 150 pounds more.

Several months after we made the pact to keep our clean laundry story in our "dirty laundry" pile, we did confess it to a few friends. As expected, they didn't ridicule us, take back loving hands from helping lift us up, and walk out of the room. I don't remember exact words said, although there definitely was incredulous laughter. I remember feeling freed to tell more people as the story resurfaced through the years, unwrapping the many packages while sitting on the floor, trying to sort the clothes and put them back in drawers and closets. Clean for now, waiting to be reused, resoiled, and then rewashed.

I sat down somewhere in the middle, and I waved her in, too. She moved slowly in among the blue package towers and snuggled in next to me. I remember the smell of sweat and Eucerin. I remember that we vowed to tell no one. I remember that the afternoon became evening before we moved again. I remember that we were both smiling.

Communion

Imagine having that white tableclothed reminder in our home's entryway. A loaf of French bread, a wine glass filled. Every morning, on the way to making livings, husband and wife must take, eat, drink. Forgiveness: choose, accept. Evenings before bed, tear, dip, swallow. Years mature, jobs change, homes grow, children arrive. Hourly, the table invites. Imagine it remained dynamic, not as religious shrine, but as means of survival, even abundance in our brokenness. Imagine it as Jesus sitting at our feet, the last, Passover supper. Offering himself. How could we look into his eyes, refuse the elements, and not partake?

Quasimo-toes

The Hunchback of Notre Dame lives in my shoes.
My Quasimo-*toes*.
Fourth in line, elongated,
frightening hunchback digits.
Freakishly conspicuous,
curving my shoes a half size longer.
Before now, I despised Quasimo-toes.
Did I inherit these from Mom's own
unreconciled trodden paths?

I wonder this, kissing my newborn's feet,
staring at brilliant, teeny toes.
No clear evidence
she'll endure these noble savages
I'd grown to spurn.
Nevertheless,
            though I may not have stayed the "straight and narrow"
on My journey,
it has been redeemed.
My unsaid prayer is that if she gets Quasimo-toes,
they'll be her legacy, not a curse.

TheNext Miracle

From: Ella deCastro Baron <edecastrobaron@yahoo.com>
To: <rollonyoubears99@yahoo.com>
Date: Wed, December 17, 2008 3:30 pm
Subject: BFF Reboot?

Hey, been trying to write this e-mail to send you. Got the kids--duh, but can't wait another three months. Many mistakes--typingw/ one hand. Baby Samaria sleeping on my chest. Asa eating macn cheese , watching "WowWow Wubbzy"--latest "favorite movie in the world." Move –hop--over Max n Ruby. Gotta love his three year old personality.

Too much to do before leaving SD. Drive to Bay Area is too long--Lord, help the kids sleep deeply. Chris swears this is the last midnight drive. it sickens him how much caffeine he has to suck down to stay alert. I feel bad that I can't help drive too much, but my body still doesn't belobg to me,not until Sami decides to stop nursing. I wanted to go a year and then have her weaned, but she's still going for it at14 mos. Apparently she didn't get my memo. Don't want to ever drink caffeine again anyway, not since I stopped cold turk' when we became vegans in '02. Even tho' both pregnancies and post partum were soooo friggin challenging--never thought I couldbe this tapped out and yet still have needs to meet (without a choice--it is a joy and honor to provide, but c'mon--I was hallucinating while nursing the first several weeksw/ Asa! Hey--'member when Patience volunteered to get me out of my Environmental Sci final by hiding in the bathroom and throwing up for me then telling my T.A. she saw a student getting sick…is she by chance in your class?! Masterful "Incomplete"grade, that one. I still can't believe we pulled it off.) No more "I" grade way out these days. I was starting to say, I'm amazed and relieved that my skin has never returned to sickness. in fact, my skin got less dry! But helloo, let's not talk abt my grey hairs that I never had before…

At leastwe were able to buy a used minivan--the "golden eagle" to Asa. Thank gawd Chris understood we can't do 10 hour road trips in our Element anymore--totally bumpy four wheel drive,absolutely no room for me to sit back there when both children were howling, screeching, sobbng, then barfing. Babies are a tad more fussy than two longboards on a long drive... thanks for the heads up, Honda! Last trip to the "V", we made it--5 a.m. --our nieces asleep on the couch, waiting. Their ten foot tree still lit for Asa to see (our puny potted 3-foot tree entertainedhim only while he ran amok in Target's garden center to choose it. there's no room to stick presents under it anyway.

Chris is still new to the Chrstian-Filipino ways around the season-- table full of lumpia, pancit, frid rice, sticky rice desserts next to barely touchedPillsbury chocolate chip cookies--made for him and the Americanized kids who also can't understand the hype from sticky coconut rice. it's purely emotional for us, conjures growing up in more uncomplicated times. The American recipe turkey has to share spotlight w/ crowds of more familiar dishes (for us brown folk--but I did try to make latkes once to go w/ spam one morning!). he still picks at the desserts-- doesn't think any rice is tasty--at least he pretends to eat it and honors us for making it. He still holds the record for consecutivelumpias in his mouth, tho'. The cousins love it--the guapo, white husband is applauded for indulgence. He's an even bigger star, andit helps them leave him off the hook when he hides for karaoke hour--he totally hates it and can't pretend he enjoys it. I sing badly enuf for both of us.

I thought we might be ready to help distribute towels and socks to the homeless in SF Christmas day this year, help my our Até Sharon w/ her yearly ministry (they're up to 10,000 pairs of sox & thousands of towels). The baby is only a year though--too cold out there for her in the early morning? Asa would really learn how to treat everyone w/ compassion,plus he's so friendly, always checking to seeif kids at the park or in the store who look upset are okay. he's always up for these adventures. Light years ahead of how shy I was growing up. If it doesn't work out this time, maybe next year. They can go more often w/ us here in SD to the church Branch meals for those on the "outside" at Mission Beach. We have to start going again. Gotta be more consistent w/ that. Don'rt want our kids to grow up sheltered, out of touch.

argh--the baby's a furnace on me (remember thefootball game one year when you kept saying it wasso hot, it was like you were"sitting on the sun?") My thighs are cramping from sittibg still. Asa's f;licked his pasta everywhere--that's wwhat I get for letting him use chopstix while I ignore him. sometimes, I think abt when I might get a free hand? theluxury to only think of myself again for longer than a quick shower once a week? shoot--what's it going to be like when I go back to teaching more part-time classes? Already had too many papers to grade before kids (same ole excuses plus real ones now). Okay--don't think too hard about how it might be. we need to pay the mortgage, and kids don't get cheaper as the grow up. could besomuch worse--no job atall, yeah? Oops--we still haven't unloaded our condo. Economy=scurry. Imagine if I hadn't finished (almost didn't, sigh--thankya Lawd that bridge is crossed and that valley a speck in the distance!) I'm really glad my degree and years in the direction of teaching has secured me some part-time way to help our family.

Now tho', I see our Greatest career call--the one we couldn't possibly train for or prep for ahead of time. Remember Kristine's quote: "Having children is God's way of raising two generations at once." amen sistah. And I already have post-partum amnesia and admit I can have or adopt a third child soon? that's either insanity catching up afterall these years, or it's outrageous, bubbilicious optimism--a hope that doesn't get its blueprints from human hearts. alien, supernatch stuff m'dear.

I feel like there are new doors opening fr us to raise our families while being true to our full identities. At least today, teaching and some writing are in the mosaic w/ wife and mom. Then, so are the eczema, and the cancer in both our families--yeah? the divorces too. But at least now, my perspective is where I've beenwanting it to be forever. I mean, these traumas are still around me, but I don't feel paralyzed by them now. Oh-- did I updateyou about Carolyn? Her eczema's just like mine--going on year 3, triggered around her wedding, all over her body, too (eerie similarities, even quit her job & is in the same community w/ some of the same peeps when we were sick). And Jennie--OMG I'm still sad for our friends--I could barely accept it for the first six months--divorce finalized on Election Day (talk about history…).

(I'm flashing back to when I ws still sick and at one of the Fri prayer mtgs. For Amelia's cancer. It was the first time I had total rage about ALL the illnesses--mine, hers, my mom's--and during the prayer time, all I could do

that hour was sob. Then something in me was done--as in emptied out--
and there was none of that anger left to eat at me. I moved to a new plane.
I wasn't raging because of how devastated I felt. I felt like that vacancy was
filled w/ seeds of the kind of faith that can grow. Plus, I was now angry at
the rightful culprit, the Sickness (maybe this is what they mean by "holy
anger"?). I stopped blaming people, circumstances, God. I started to take
my share of responsibility to stand shoulder to shoulder w/ others and take
back everything that's been ripped away from us. I was seeing my enemy
eye to eye, and even though I had just a slingshot against the Giant, I'd
already been told how that story ends!)

I'm just pissed now more than afraid or resigned. These are not their or
anyone's fates--we can contend for complete restoration from all of it.
And the don't have to wait as long as we did to really really seek after
wholeness (& abundant life). Like--halleloo-Yeah--my mom's been a breast
cancer survivor going on six years. It shook & woke her up. She retired
fr. Kaiser last yr. They built a home in the P.I., help plant churches there,
raise donations when they're in Vallejo half the year. We miss them (I was
bummed the kids don't get to really spend time w/ their lola), but I don't
think she could be more of who she Is.

Anyway, back to Carolyn. We've already been praying for Carolyn & Tyson
(we have so much empathy for his burden as her husband--how isolated
and exhausted he gets too), and there have been great breakthroughs.
We're waiting in confidence for her skin to be 100% new. I have no doubt
it can and does happen, so when her days are darkest, and shes curled up
at home totally despairing, it doesn't faze me when she sends out an SOS.
Still learning how to discern how to pray and what to do each specific time,
but from these last many years and what I've seen/been witness to, there's
no more doubt. I *KNOW* God can heal. Been dere, done dat!

I don't have the specific process Jennie has to endure, BUT I know she
isn't designed to be alone. BTW, haveyou talked lately? She's been taking
short trips here and there, but she's settling back to work, applying to
PhD school. She just visited Costa Rica--sent us a postard from a tropical
butterfly sanctuary. She wrote she's focusing on the "after cocoon season."
I know she'll come out of this the butterfly she is--the best part of this
transformation is that a caterpillar doesn't have to "earn" the cocoon and
then its "wings"(ha). It's part of the creature's intrinsic design. So cool to
think we've got these deposits of glory in waiting.

As out of control as it can feel, I have assurance that my vision is always being refined. Big time--like the diamonds that come from immense pressure and chipping away at the coal. Remember? (denim & diamonds... LOL) You used to say when we had our "planned nervous breakdowns"in undergrad that we never know which chink that's crumbling us is the one that reveals brilliance (is this an insensitive metaphor b/c of blood diamonds...cut to me sliding my diamond ring around to hide tha ice...!? you get the point.)

Finally, baby's stirring, and Asa wants more juice in his Diego cup. Wonder if I'll get to go to the gym this week. who am I kidding? this month. I wanna call Chris--will he p/u Rubios after work. craving fish taco especiale. hungryyyy.jk;;kjb;ui/klnnnnnnnn she sat on keypad. lbbbbbbb/jjj

+++++++++

OKAY--Chris just came home early--surprised me--wants us to take the kids to the neighborhood park. I have a few seconds while he puts their shoes on. I rambled, but I also wanted to tell you I finished my CV. Finally--as final as it gets (for now). It's fuller than I thought it ever could be, and I know it's going to constantly be in progress. As painful as it often was, and as battle weary as I found myself--more than I thought and actually could bear at the time, until Chris and the rest of you guys picked me up--the intermittent victories, the barrel-scraping-bottom defeats, and the overall journey revealed and developed a "skill set" I can stand on for a good while. Cross your fingers that it'll find me that career position!

I'm attaching it here for your opinion since you're one of my longest (not oldest...self-proclaimed "spring chicken") and most faithful friends (plus you've been on so much of this adventure with me). On our drive back down from Vallejo, let's try to converge our paths. I know I've been MIA, but I miss our times together. Since I'm still skin and spirit-healthy, maybe we can go to the beach--gotta love SoCal's winters! You can be naked with Ugh-*ly* boots on and be just foine (I still can't get used to those furry loaves of footbread). You have to see how even funnier Asa is, and the baby is getting her slapstick on, too.

Honestly, I never thought Life could be like this. Most days, tired beyond recognition. Yet, filled beyond comprehension. Could we have predicted this back in the day while walking up the hill to the House to get ready to "study" in the Suitor's room?!

I can't wait to hear about your time living and working overseas. Saw your Facebook photos already; just need the voiceovers now! Serve up the juicier stories, too--lemme take a bite out of those!

Let's call/text each other. My number's the same.

peace.

~E

Credits

The following pieces have been previously published and are reprinted here with permission.

"First Miracle," "Heads Up, Seven Up," "Another Grandfather Poem," "Jesus Action Figure," and "Homemade Café" are published in past issues of *CityWorks Literary Journal,* City Works Press.

"Café du Monde" is published in *Hunger and Thirst Food Literature*, City Works Press.

"weather forecast" is published in *Sunshine/Noir*, City Works Press.

"Kaua'i" is published in *Fictional International* #38, San Diego State University Press.

Itchy Brown Girl
Seeks Employment

ELLA DECASTRO BARON

Ella deCastro Baron is a first generation Filipina American born in Oakland and raised in Vallejo, California. With a BA in English Literature from UC Berkeley, Ella moved to San Diego to earn a Master of Fine Arts degree in Creative Writing. She is a full-time wife and mother of two little ones, a part-time English and Creative Writing instructor at San Diego City College, and an "other"-times published writer in publications such as *Fiction International, Sunshine Noir, and CityWorks Literary Journal.* She hopes to continue being a witness to her ethnic upbringing, her faith, her interracial family, and how it may or may not fit together. This is her first book.